MOST COLLEGE STUDENTS ARE WOMEN

Also available in the Women in Academe series:

The Balancing Act:
Gendered Perspectives in Faculty Roles and Work Lives

Women in Academic Leadership:
Professional Strategies, Personal Choices

MOST COLLEGE

STUDENTS ARE WOMEN

Implications for Teaching, Learning, and Policy

Edited by

Jeanie K. Allen, Diane R. Dean,

and Susan J. Bracken

Foreword by *David Sadker*

STERLING, VIRGINIA

COPYRIGHT © 2008 BY STYLUS PUBLISHING, LLC.

Published by Stylus Publishing, LLC
22883 Quicksilver Drive
Sterling, Virginia 20166–2102

Library of Congress Cataloging-in-Publication-Data
Most college students are women : implications for teaching, learning, and policy / edited by Jeanie K. Allen, Susan J. Bracken, and Diane R. Dean ; foreword by David Sadker.—1st ed.

    p.   cm.

    Includes bibliographical references and index.

    ISBN 978-1-57922-190-4 (cloth : alk. paper)—ISBN 978-1-57922-191-1 (pbk. : alk. paper)

    1. Women—Education (Higher)—United States.   2. Women college students—United States.   3. Sexism in higher education—United States.   I. Allen, Jeanie K., 1951–   II. Bracken, Susan J.   III. Dean, Diane R., 1967–

    LC1756.M67   2008

    378.0082—dc22   2008025789

13-digit ISBN: 978–1–57922–190–4 (cloth)
13-digit ISBN: 978–1–57922–191–1 (paper)

Printed in the United States of America

All first editions printed on acid free paper
that meets the American National Standards Institute
Z39–48 Standard.

Bulk Purchases

Quantity discounts are available for use in workshops and for staff development.
Call 1–800–232–0223

First Edition, 2008

10 9 8 7 6 5 4 3 2 1

CONTENTS

v

ACKNOWLEDGMENTS

This project would not have been possible without the hard work and support of many people who believe in and work toward equity issues for students in higher education. We sincerely appreciate everything you do! We especially want to thank John von Knorring, Judy Coughlin, Karen Haley, Mary Dee Wenniger, and, of course, all of the contributing authors.

Jeanie Allen

I would like to thank my husband, Charlie, for his constant encouragement. Special thanks also to my mother, Ann Kattan, for cheering me on throughout my life; and to my daughter Hilary for reminding me during her college years how women's experience still differs from men's. In addition, I would like to thank all of the women I had the privilege of meeting through Women's Caucus of the American Association of Higher Education, as well as all of the women who have been friends, colleagues, and mentors in my life.

Diane Dean

I would like to thank my husband, John Giglio, for his support and encouragement. Thank you also to Norma Burgess, Katie Embree, Joseph Hankin, Arthur Levine, Sharon McDade, Elizabeth Miller, and the many members of the Women's Caucus of the American Association of Higher Education, whose friendship and mentoring I value greatly. This volume grew out of our collective mission and vision for equity in academe.

Sue Bracken

Thank you to my family—Jeff, Trish, and Laura—and also to Trish, Jay, Erica, and Evan for their love and support. And a thank-you to my former and current colleagues whose presence in my work life has made a positive, lasting impact. You are terrific.

FOREWORD

David Sadker

Let me begin by recalling my Bronx boyhood and sharing a meaningful quotation from Yogi Berra, a catcher for the New York Yankees who practiced philosophy without a license: "If you come to a fork in the road, take it." This book is all about people who saw forks in the road that others missed, educators who saw educational choices while others saw only one path with no choices. The wonderful contributors to this collection are really sharing their own life experiences and their own insights into making college classrooms responsive to female students. Oh, I know, "Women are already the majority of college students, what are you talking about?" Regardless of whether women are in the majority, many colleges still have a very male feel, a mostly male professorship, and administrators and presidents who continue a male culture both in and beyond the classroom. Many administrators and professors try to make the campus "female friendly," but they often fall short. This book is all about helping them succeed.

Let me share a personal story or two about my encounters with sexism on campus. My late wife, Myra, and I met at Harvard, both students in the Master of Arts in Teaching program. It was a secret to no one that Myra was a strong student, receiving top grades and doing a terrific job teaching her middle school classes. I was no slouch, but if GPAs were to be believed, Myra was doing better. On a beautiful night in Cambridge, the education honor society held a formal induction of new members, students recognized for their achievements. That would be me; Myra watched from the sidelines. I was inducted and Myra was not, because women were barred. In the mid-1960s, the honor society was termed an honor "fraternity." Although Phi Delta Kappa had no frat house, no party schedule, not much of anything that would say "This is a fraternity," that is what it was called. Forget her better grades, Myra failed Gender 101, and we were both learning about the "old boys' network."

The situation never sat well with either of us, so over the next few years we spent some of our time protesting the gender bias in Phi Delta Kappa, and through the hard work of many people, the honorary fraternity eventually became an honorary society. Myra was then admitted, almost a decade later. Such sexist policies are unfamiliar to many of today's students, students who seem more cognizant of the history of racism than they are of the sex discrimination that accompanied it for centuries. Looking back, Phi Delta Kappa was a piece of cake or, better yet, a piece of blatant bias that took only a spotlight to vanquish. The sexist policies that kept women out of honorary groups, courses and programs, and many colleges, including the Ivy League, would one day tumble under public scrutiny. Today, it is the more subtle stuff that eludes us.

Here is an example of the more subtle challenges. A few years after that memorable induction night at Harvard, we decided to try education at the other end of Massachusetts, in Amherst, this time working on our doctorates. We studied hard and wrote well together, even coauthoring several articles and proposals. People were impressed with our productivity and our insights, but they had an unusual way of expressing it. They would refer to our writings as "David's work." In this shorthand, Myra became invisible yet again. When we pointed out the problem, people would explain, "When we say David, we really mean David and Myra." That didn't work for either of us. The experience opened our eyes to another dimension of sexism in the academy, the subtle power of speech and word choice to diminish females.

Myra felt awful, and so did I, but Myra decided to do something about it. It was one of those decisions that seemed important on the personal level, a little frightening in the real world, where consequences could follow, but the right thing to do. She wrote an editorial in the school paper (a mimeographed informal paper with a circulation of a few hundred) describing how it felt to work hard and be ignored because she was a woman, and how unfair that such a culture thrived in a school of education committed to social justice. As chance would have it (was it chance or was something bigger at work?), a professor who was doing a series of books for Harper and Row read Myra's one-page editorial and invited her to write a book about what happens to girls in school. A book! From 1969 to 1971, Myra worked on *Sexism in School and Society* (1973), one of the very first books focusing on girls in school. While Myra went off to the library (you actually had to go to libraries back then to research books!), I was at home caring for our only daughter at the time. Myra's book was quite an eye-opener. Other books about gender issues in school had always focused on boys: *Why Johnny Can't Read, The Feminization of Boys,* and the like. Boys had discipline problems and struggled in reading and other areas, and those books confronted those well-known problems. Girls' problems fell below the radar. Myra described how neatly dressed young girls who were staying out of trouble were in reality paying a high price for their high grades. They were learning to be docile and obedient, to conform, to lose their independence and their public voices. They were being educated for second-class citizenship in the workplace and beyond.

Myra's editorial and book set us both on a path of researching and writing to uncover gender bias and create more equitable relationships in school and beyond. In an early study, we content analyzed teacher education textbooks, books used to prepare new teachers. We wanted to see how such books treated issues like gender and women's experiences. We found that these textbooks gave little space or attention to the many contributions of women in the field of teaching, did almost nothing to alert new teachers to the issue of gender bias in their classrooms, and sometimes recommended sexist teaching strategies. For example, teachers were being told to stock their bookshelves with books with male characters and stories, because boys are only interested in reading about boys, and girls will read anything. One thing I have learned over the years—which is kind of sad—is that even when one of these areas gets "corrected," you have to track it all the time. Even today, such sexist teaching ideas are still being promoted. A few years ago, I redid that teacher textbook study. After thirty years, I discovered that sex bias is still a significant problem in teacher education texts. Not as bad as before, but still a problem. Gender bias has many lives.

Myra and I spent a number of years investigating how teachers interact with female and male students. We looked at hundreds of classrooms, in college and in elementary and secondary schools, discovering similar patterns at all levels of American education. Boys are more likely to speak up and more likely to be called on in class, they receive more positive and more negative teacher comments, and they are more likely to act out in class and receive more active help from the teacher. Girls are less likely to speak up or be called on and are more likely to be silent in class, spectators to their own education. Girls are pleased with their grades, and their teachers certainly appreciate their good behavior, but in the end it is a sad trade-off. They are being rewarded for docility, conformity, and obedience, for following the rules and knowing their place. They are losing their public voice, and in their adult life, these lessons of second-class citizenship are costly. My observations today, although more informal, tend to reinforce our original findings, that gender-biased patterns still dominate many classrooms. Little has been done over the years to correct these imbalances.

There seems to be an endless need for books like *Most College Students Are Women*, because unless we continue reminding academe of gender bias, it quickly takes root. For example, in the past decade even the word "feminism" has been misappropriated. To me, "feminism" means equality between the sexes, a concept that recalls that "all people are created equal." Who would have thought that the founding concept of our nation would be controversial and threatening? In class last semester, I asked my students what they thought of feminism. One young woman responded, "I really think this gender equity has gone too far." That is a phrase I hear over and over in class, "gone too far," or "I am for equal rights, but this is too much." So I asked the student to give me an example. She said that she read about "a woman who sued so that she could be a sheriff and guard prisoners in court. A few months later she was guarding a prisoner who took away her gun and killed her and other people. To me, that's an example of feminism going too far." That's where many students are today, seeing one woman's error as confirmation that all women stand accused. One would have to explain the double standard to this student, that most prisoners escape from male guards; so would she conclude that we should not have male guards? That is a nineteen-year-old's view of feminism today, all very disconcerting but a clear reason why books such as this one are important vehicles to connect with today's college students, to bring gender issues into the light.

How does gender influence learning? The authors in this collection come from a variety of perspectives as they explore gender in higher education. From the importance of relationships in learning to the frontier of neuroscience, the authors open doors, pose questions, and sometimes suggest answers for those working in higher education. During the 1980s, *In a Different Voice* and *Women's Ways of Knowing* became cult symbols to legitimize and explain female thoughts and experiences. As a reviewer in *Vogue* enthused about Carol Gilligan's *In a Different Voice*, "It is impossible to consider Gilligan's ideas without having your estimation of women rise."[1] The problem was no longer that females were overly emotional and illogical but that their experiences and approaches to the world should be honored, not degraded.

Feminist pedagogy has taught us important lessons, but I believe that they are lessons that go beyond gender. Women's experiences—in fact, all our experiences—need to be recognized and honored in (and beyond) schools. Too often they are not, as we are taught the "right way" to see things and do things, and that "right way" is too often a Western, male perspective. But males are not all the same, and sometimes they too are silenced in school. We need to learn how to invite all voices to be heard, those new to English, quiet girls, and quiet boys. It is not just *women's ways of knowing*, it is each one of us who has a way of knowing, of learning, of seeing the world. Those multiple ways of knowing, learning, and being enrich the human experience and should all be part of the school experience. Feminists have given us an enduring lesson, a lesson of connection, of learning from one another and not simply from an authority figure or in a competitive climate. Schools and colleges need to work harder to follow the feminist lead and explore multiple ways of teaching and learning in the academy.

Alvin Toffler, author of *Future Shock*, likens what is taught in school to driving a car with your eyes glued to the rearview mirror. Schools and colleges too often teach about yesterday rather than for tomorrow. Daniel Pink, in his book *A Whole New Mind: Why Right-Brainers Will Rule the Future*, builds on this hypothesis and is concerned with schools' traditional emphasis on teaching logic, the scientific method, and other left-brain learning. Pink makes the case that India can do left-brain work far cheaper than we can, that computers can do left-brain work faster than we can, and that the part of the brain on which schools should be focusing is the creative part, the artistic part, in short, the right brain. We need to investigate new ways of teaching, of learning, of seeing the world.

The ideas and approaches in *Most College Students Are Women* offer perspectives that help us unravel the cultural blinders that limit our vision. I think it was Beverly Tatum who said that everybody should be inoculated against racism every day, because every day we inhale it. I think it is the same with sexism: Every day you breathe it in without even knowing. It is like smoke, a passive bias. We need to see and eliminate sexism and racism, but what we really need to do is find a broader framework, something bigger than gender or race or the other labels that we use. Certain cultural labels have become salient, like race and gender, while others have not. Our culture might have seen right-handed people or tall people or heavy people as the critical groupings, but it did not. All such labels divide and diminish us, because it is not our outside package that should declare who or what we are to the world; we should all be valued for what we bring to the world, our inner gifts. I want to skip over the place where we look to skin color, religion, race, or gender and instead see the person. I think we need a bolder way of dealing with these issues, with our humanity, and with our souls. I am not saying that we should be treating everyone the same, or pretending that the world does not have racism or sexism or classism. Of course it does, but I want to get beyond what our eyes see to what we do not see, which is often more important. We need to think more about how we honor, or do not honor, one another.

Former senator Bill Bradley recently wrote a book called *The New American Story,* in which he asks the reader to consider what makes us proud to be Americans. Does it make us proud that we are so rich, that someday we may have a million millionaires in our country? Are we proud to have such wealth yet tolerate crippling poverty? Are we proud to be driving huge SUVs, bigger cars than any other people drive? We have the most powerful army in the world—does that make us proud (or secure)? Bradley talks about the unseen, the inner souls of people that in fact do make us proud. For me, I remember the Virginia Tech shootings, that tragedy that stunned our nation. Yet I felt pride seeing that campus community pull together, hearing of a teacher sacrificing himself to save his students' lives. I watched that moving Hokie candlelight vigil, and I could almost feel the unseen spirit of that institution being reborn. Bradley tells the story of a shoeshine guy in Pittsburgh, a man who worked near a children's hospital, where every day he saw children too poor to pay for treatment. That shoeshine man decided to split his tips in half and donate one half to a fund for the treatment of those poor children. He donated $150,000 to the hospital to help those kids: a shoeshine man! That is what makes me proud. Is that shoeshine man Black or White? I do not know. Would it matter if it were a woman or a Latino? No, because we all value the human soul.

Nelson Mandela, in his inaugural speech, used a Marianne Williamson quotation that I love: "Our deepest fear is not that we are inadequate. Our deepest fear is that we are powerful beyond measure. It is our light, not our darkness, that most frightens us." We must move beyond traditional frameworks that too often limit the human spirit. This book begins that journey of honoring students who learn differently, but well, and of honoring the sacred human spirit that we all share.

Notes

1. *Vogue* review quoted on book jacket of Carol Gilligan, *In a Different Voice* (Cambridge, MA: Harvard University Press, 1982).

INTRODUCTION

WOMEN LEARNERS ON CAMPUS
What Do We Know and What Have We Done?

Jeanie K. Allen, Diane R. Dean, and Susan J. Bracken

This book constitutes the third, and final, volume in the Women in Academe series. We, the coeditors, owe the origination of this series to our involvement as past chairs of the former American Association for Higher Education's Women's Caucus. The caucus provided women in colleges and universities a place to learn and share research and professional development. The rich friendships and exciting research that came out of this organization inspired us to preserve and continue the work of the members. It was from our collaboration as chairs that we entertained the idea of publishing these three texts. As members of the caucus, we realized that we shared concerns about our lives as researchers, faculty, and students. Thus, our project, Women in Academe: Scholars, Leaders, and Learners, was initiated.

The Balancing Act (Bracken, Allen, & Dean, 2006), the first volume in the series, examined women's lives as faculty members, noting the barriers that appear to obstruct women's pathway to tenure. The second volume, *Women in Academic Leadership* (Dean, Bracken, & Allen, in press) sought to present research regarding the underrepresentation of women in administrative positions, illuminating challenges and experiences from successful women administrators at all levels. This third and final volume features a collection of studies regarding the current status of research on women's experiences as learners in higher education.

Women as Learners in Higher Education

For at least the past 40 years, the majority of students in higher education have been women. Women of all ages sought, and continue to seek, the rewards of postsecondary degrees. As more female students arrived on campuses, questions emerged about discriminatory policies; a seemingly masculine environment, curriculum, and pedagogy; and equal funding. These questions led to a variety of important research projects and a rich array of publications. This book contains recent works that build on this body of research. Thus, we begin by examining a few of the scholars who originated these queries.

As we, the coeditors, began to discuss the major overarching themes that arise from the increasing female population in higher education, we settled on three: the different perspectives that emerge when women become the focus of research, the different voice that may be present when discussing women's styles of learning, and the different pedagogical strategies that might be considered when examining classrooms largely made up of female learners. Therefore, we begin this volume with a brief examination of three major works relevant to understanding women students: *Toward a New Psychology of Women* (Miller, 1976/1986); *Women's Ways of Knowing: The Development of Self, Voice, and Mind* (Belenky, Clinchy, Goldberger, & Tarule, 1986/1997); and *Failing at Fairness: How Our Schools Cheat Girls* (Sadker & Sadker, 1994).

Is There a Psychology of Women?

In 1976, after years of clinical practice and study of the research methods common to previous eras, Jean Baker Miller (1976/1986) asked, does the data provide the whole picture, or are we studying women in the context of men's lives (Allen, 2002)? She proposed that historically most researchers were male; men had been used as the subjects of most research; and, thus, men's lives became the norms by which all members of society were judged. In addition, Miller asserted that a major component of Western culture involves the assignment of roles of either dominant or subordinate status, which in turn creates institutions that promote permanent inequality. Miller concluded that judging women against male norms and defining as subordinate their often required role as caretaker placed women at a permanent disadvantage.

Miller's (1976/1986) description of the characteristics of women that evolved from the role of subordinate included cooperation, attunement to others' needs, fostering growth in others, and creativity born out of surviving in a culture that devalued their contributions. She then proposed that perhaps it was time to examine these traits as strengths rather than weaknesses, even suggesting that it was these very traits that might provide benefit in the future more than the celebrated traits of competition, winning, self-interest, and control. The concepts of power and conflict needed to be rethought, according to Miller, and women appeared to avoid discussing either of these subjects. Miller emphasized that power could be redefined as power with, rather than power over, others and that conflict must be seen as enhancing development, not diminishing identity, as is often seen when dominant persons engage in disputes with subordinates.

Miller's (1976/1986) work applies directly to a historical perspective of higher education. Male norms set the standards for entrance requirements, the out-of-class environment and traditions, the traditional curriculum, and pedagogy in the classroom. In addition, the subordinate role assigned to "women's issues" resulted in fewer resources and less attention paid to fields that tended to be more female dominated. Aggressive competition, choosing the self over others, and individual achievement regardless of the context dominated the classroom. Perhaps Miller was correct. Higher education had opened the doors of opportunity for women, but only if they chose to live their lives under masculine definitions.

Do Women Learn Differently?

Ten years after Miller (1976/1986) published her text, Belenky et al. (1986/1997) began asking similar questions about learning theory. Again, past works had used essentially all male subjects, setting standards based on men's lives. These four researchers investigated cognitive development using a variety of women as the subjects of their study. Their conclusions opened the doors to a view of a different pathway through the learning process.

Whereas the male-based models of cognitive development emphasized autonomy and objectivity, Belenky et al. (1986/1997) found a tendency for women to value relationships, listening, and connection, suggesting a different perspective on knowledge and knowing. The authors noted that women learners seemed to prefer different relationships with knowledge and authorities than most male students did. Female students seemed to favor listening as a mode of learning, defining their learning modes in relationship to others, not separate from others, as the masculine model suggested. In addition, because the majority of authorities in higher education tended to be male, with a masculine approach to teaching and learning, the women students respected their knowledge but did not carry the same level of desire to model the "expert" as did their male counterparts. Instead, most female learners sought to find their own "voice" in the educational experience. The masculine norms greeted these learners with aggressive competition and debate, suggesting that winning people over was a primary goal in higher education. Women learners, on the other hand, sought to understand others' points of view, continuing to validate Miller's (1976/1986) suggestions that many women learn best when involved in cooperating with and developing others.

Women's Ways of Knowing (Belenky et al., 1986/1997) opened the door to further consideration of classroom environment, pedagogy, and the role of authority in the classroom. Over time, higher education has experienced a surge in the use of active and cooperative learning, narrative as a form of expression and knowledge, and a more diverse representation of texts in the classroom. Questions remained, however, about the actual practice of the authorities (professors) in the classroom.

Do Professors Favor Males in the Classroom?

Myra and David Sadker (1994) produced groundbreaking research about gender bias in classrooms. They found that at all levels of education, the classroom experience for males and females differed significantly. In class texts, if women were mentioned, it was usually an insert or a "special box," placing women's contributions as secondary and lesser to men's. With regard to language, the continuous use of "he" to represent everyone appeared to be accepted by both students and teachers. Male students tended to monopolize classroom discussions and were called on by name more often than female students. When males had made comments, their comments were expounded on or referred back to more often than were the contributions made by female students. When criticizing student work, teachers tended to ask questions of the men, requiring them to think about their work, or provided concrete suggestions for improvement, whereas they simply did the work for the female students. Sexist jokes and comments in class that demeaned women were ignored or, worse, condoned. Male students were praised for their accomplishments, whereas female students were acknowledged for their appearance.

With this sort of treatment in kindergarten through the senior year in high school, it is no surprise that women's views of themselves as learners differ when they arrive at the college classroom. In college classrooms, the professor is more often male, especially in science and technology departments. The Sadkers (1994) noted numerous examples of college classrooms in which professors literally demeaned women students, using and allowing sexist comments throughout the semesters. The same discriminatory practices found in K–12 education continued in the college classroom. But it is from these and other research projects too numerous to mention that the ideas of feminist pedagogy emerged.

An Inclusive Classroom

In chapter 1 of this volume, Becky Ropers-Huilman and Betsy Palmer present background material on feminist pedagogy, an approach that poses opposition to the traditional, authoritarian classroom, in which students are encouraged to accept authority and seek individual, autonomous achievement. In a feminist classroom, difference, cooperation, and challenging the status quo are encouraged. A primary component of previous research suggested that most women students prefer an integration of their personal and academic lives, using their experiences as sources of knowledge. Such an integration naturally involves interdisciplinary approaches. Rarely does one's experience fit neatly in the disciplinary boundaries that guard knowledge in higher education. In addition, identities emerge from experience; thus, there can be no one-size-fits-all approach, as is often found in a standard curriculum. Texts that minimize contributions from individuals other than White males cannot provide validation of the lived experiences of diverse students. Women's assumed role of subordination and lack of inclusion places learning in many classrooms outside their lived lives and also suggests to these learners that they need to be submissive and passive in the classroom. Education that seeks to maintain the status quo often distances students with differing viewpoints and perspective. Thus, a feminist classroom encourages students to incorporate their experiences into the knowledge base, share in the creation of knowledge, and seek social change. Although these concerns have grown out of research on women, we argue that such an approach enhances learning for all students.

Where Are We Now?

Some aspects of higher education have improved significantly for women students. Women now excel in their academic pursuits and enter graduate schools and professional programs in numbers equal to, if not greater than, their male counterparts. They graduate with honors and participate in all levels of research projects. Title IX funding has narrowed the gap in resources so that women can participate equally in academe. Women's studies programs have become prevalent, and many college faculty are immersed in eliminating gender bias. The true strength of asking questions about women learners, however, has been the emergence of a substantial body of research that helps all students. The implications of gender research affect the in-class and out-of-class experience for students at all levels of education. Each of the authors in this volume speaks from her own voice and experience, highlighting both progressive thinking that has come about through research on women learners and the barriers that remain.

In chapter 1, Becky Ropers-Huilman and Betsy Palmer extend the perceptions of feminist pedagogy by discussing the overlap between feminist pedagogy and the call for all institutions of higher education to engage in civic education. Marcia Baxter Magolda, in chapter 2, provides a model of pedagogy that incorporates different pathways that she titles "gender related." Her Learning Partnership Model expands on her research and contributes concrete suggestions for designing classes to meet all students' needs. Kathleen Taylor and Catherine Marienau, in chapter 3, demonstrate ways in which their previous research on women adult learners is now being validated by neuropsychology. These discoveries provide a strong link between the social and physical sciences, a link that shows potential in improving learning for all.

However, all barriers and challenges for women students have not been overcome. We continue to see lower enrollment for female learners in the sciences and technology fields. Teri Sosa (chapter 4) provides the latest research on this phenomenon, as well as examples of programs that recruit and retain women students in these important fields. Marilyn Simon (chapter 5) discusses the difficulties that still seem to surface for female learners in the field of statistics, suggesting a relationship to previous research on mathematics education and women. She also includes suggestions about the growing field of online learning and methods that enhance women's success in that venue.

The intersection of gender and race presents another barrier for women, and men, students. Crystal Gafford Muhammad and Adrienne Dixson (chapter 6) describe the results of classroom exercises designed to engage students in understanding the role that race plays in the learning environment and society. The cocurricular environment continues to promote a subordinate and passive role for women students, and Jeanie K. Allen (chapter 7) examines this seemingly "chilly" out-of-class experience through the lens of developmental models. She provides suggestions that schools might consider to improve the out-of-class experience for all students. Susan J. Bracken (chapter 8) ends this volume with a discussion about teaching women's studies in the context of adult learning as a field of study. She examines the idea of submerged feminism as she elaborates on the adult learner's tendency to state, "I'm not a feminist, but . . ."

This volume cannot possibly do justice to all the scholars who have engaged in research on women and higher education. These chapters do not present the broad array of significant contributions being made by scholars all over the world regarding the role of gender in society. Our purpose was to create a brief volume of a variety of works dedicated to enhancing the learning environment for women students, a project that in turn improves higher education for all students. In keeping with our feminist backgrounds, we chose an array of researchers at all levels in academe and also have maintained their "voice" in each of the following chapters. It is our intention that this volume provide only a snapshot of the issues facing women students in higher education, and, ultimately, we hope that the readers finish this text by asking their own set of questions in order to embark on research paths to improve learning for all in academe.

Suggestions for Building Awareness, Advocacy and Action

In keeping with *The Balancing Act* and *Women in Academic Leadership*, we again would like to offer concrete suggestions for faculty and policymakers seeking to provide optimal educational experiences for women and, better yet, for all students. These suggestions require us to step out of our own roles and see our educational practices from the perspective of our students.

Awareness

1. Maintain vigilant awareness of campus work lives, environments, and practices and question what we define and accept as normal. In addition to asking how this collection of research and writing confirms or differs from the experiences that we live or observe on our own campuses, we can also ask ourselves why we participate in shaping imbalanced or inequitable workplace practices and learning environments, and what this models to our students. Do we ourselves need to ask whether our institution presents an inequitable set of practices that we actively or passively condone? What actions could we take?

2. Reflect on what we and our campuses identify as appropriate educational practices and desired outcomes from our curriculum and courses. Many courses and texts continue to devalue the contributions of women as scholars and leaders. Do we continue to send overt and covert messages to women students that we are simply preparing them for lives that continue their subordination and underrepresentation?

3. Maintain awareness of multiple dimensions of identity and their intersections. As we continue to understand and challenge the barriers that limit opportunities for women in academe, we must remain aware of other dimensions of identity that constrain or enable individual choices and actions. Strategies and choices appropriate for one group of women may be inadequate for another. Racial, religious, socioeconomic, and other differences necessitate different strategies and compel different choices.

Advocacy

4. Embrace the "personal is political" in your work and look for it in the work of others. Equitable, healthy work environments, viewed and framed as good for women, are also good for all members of the campus community and essential for the longevity of the academy. Our work environments influence students' perceptions of what is fair and equitable. Students learn both in and out of the classroom. We can and should be critically reflective of our own and others' participation, leadership, and agency in creating positive and equitable learning environments.

5. Balance the process of problem identification with inquiry into note-worthy positive structures and practices. In *The Balancing Act,* we cautioned against focusing exclusively on identifying and labeling problems within the academy and on viewing solutions as lying outside ourselves and residing in actions that others should take instead. We can become solution seekers, asking ourselves what are the best practices on our campuses and elsewhere for developing women students to their highest potential and what more may be achieved on our own campuses. What kinds of environments and practices would model lives that we want for our women students?

Action

6. Reenvision ourselves as adult learners in addition to experts in our respective fields. In *The Balancing Act* we made an appeal for academics to perceive themselves as lifelong adult learners in need of ongoing personal and professional opportunities to grow and learn. Here we suggest that faculty and staff receive ongoing professional development regarding new research on learning theory and pedagogical practices for women learners and for all students. Most institutions suggest in their mission statements that diversity is a crucial component in preparing students for their futures; however, attention needs to be paid to addressing that diversity in our classrooms and cocurricular offerings.

7. Act. Feminist pedagogy grew out of activist organizations. We suggest that all members of academic institutions change their own practices to align with what we know most benefits our students. In addition, speaking out and working to educate others is also necessary. Challenging the status quo is never comfortable, but as feminist literature reminds us, those who benefit most from the present situation will rarely initiate change.

8. Build informal support networks. Changing perceptions and practices in higher education is challenging and often exhausting, unrewarded work. As professionals, we need collaboration and cooperation to transform our institutional norms. Such networks can also become the conduits for the collective agency necessary to change the social and organizational systems within which we live, study, and work.

As Dr. Sadker reminds us in his foreword, "When you come to a fork in the road, take it."

References

Allen, J. K. (2002). *Searching for a path: A study of transitions in female undergraduate students.* Unpublished doctoral dissertation, Walden University, Minneapolis.

Belenky, M. F., Clinchy, B. M., Goldberger, N. R., & Tarule, J. M. (1997). *Women's ways of knowing: The development of self, voice, and mind* (10th anniversary ed.). New York: Basic Books. (Originally published 1986)

Bracken, S. J., Allen, J. K., & Dean, D. R. (Eds.). (2006). *The balancing act: Gendered perspectives on faculty roles and work lives.* Sterling, VA: Stylus.

Dean, D. R., Bracken, S. J., & Allen, J. K. (Eds.). (in press). *Women in academic leadership: Professional strategies, personal choices* Sterling, VA: Stylus.

Miller, J. B. (1986). *Toward a new psychology of women* (2nd ed.). Boston: Beacon Press. (First edition published 1976)

Sadker, M., & Sadker, D. (1994). *Failing at fairness: How our schools cheat girls.* New York: Simon & Schuster.

FEMINIST AND CIVIC EDUCATION

Bridging Parallel Approaches to Teaching and Learning

Becky Ropers-Huilman and Betsy Palmer

S cholarship related to both civic education and feminist education has made substantial contributions to educators' understandings about teaching and learning relationships both within and outside higher education institutions. However, only rarely do these two bodies of knowledge explicitly draw on each other's examinations to inform the terms of their research and practice. This chapter represents one effort to posit the main themes and complexities of feminist education literature and civic education literature in order to illustrate the ways in which they could both inform and complicate each other's underlying tenets. Specifically, this chapter focuses on key values of feminist and civic education (including learning through engagement, power/empowerment, and community), as well as key strategies that are advocated in each of these scholarly literatures to enact those values.

We believe that the various approaches that educators take to their interactions with students have the potential to shape all participants in significant ways and, subsequently, to shape the larger society in which we all live. We are guided by the assumption from critical education that "education is politics because it is one place where individuals and society are constructed. Because human beings and their society are developed in one direction or another through education, the learning process cannot avoid being political" (Shor, 1993, p. 28). By examining the sometimes unspoken values underlying civic and feminist education, we hope to illuminate some of the political nuances in each tradition. In this chapter we contribute to scholarly dialogue informing both practice and research by asking, How do these two scholarly traditions, feminist and civic education, complement each other? Also, how might these two traditions challenge each other?

Feminist Education

Although feminist education takes shape in many different practices and is informed by multiple theories (Cohee et al., 1998; Maher & Tetreault, 1994; Ropers-Huilman, 1998), it can be loosely defined in the following ways: (1) "Feminist education values experiences as sources of knowing"; (2) "Feminist education values disciplinary and interdisciplinary knowledge"; (3) "Feminist education recognizes the effects that gender or other identity characteristics have on educational process and outcomes"; (4) "Feminist education recognizes power hierarchies between teachers and learners"; and (5) "Feminist education recognizes and draws attention to the role of education in social change" (Ropers-Huilman, 2002, pp. 255–257). Feminist education can be understood as an intersection of activism and academics, both serving to critique current social structures and practices and attempting to reconstruct social interactions in more equitable and fair ways.

Although the earliest roots of feminist higher education in the United States may be found in the simple arguments made in the early 1800s to allow women entrance into the otherwise exclusively male academy, the formal discussion of a specifically feminist pedagogy arose with the second wave of feminism in the late 1950s and early 1960s. Early expressions of a feminist pedagogy were topics of discussion at feminist conferences and among neophyte faculty in newly developing women's studies programs and departments (Fisher, 2001). These early discussions of a feminist approach to teaching drew from the consciousness-raising experiences of groups of women within the broader women's movement. Perhaps in part because these early discussions of feminist education were tied to this nonacademic social justice movement, they professed a critical outsider position in relation to the academy. In particular, early advocates of feminist education continually asked how and why women students (and faculty) were oppressed by traditional male-dominated academic institutions and also how feminist educators might construct an alternative learning environment "in which women, and men, can reach their full intellectual and emotional potential" (Cohee et al., 1998, p. 8). As such, early feminists within the academy constantly negotiated their position relative to the traditions of the academy, needing to be accepted within the traditional norms of the academy in order to retain their positions while at the same time remaining critical of those norms (Fisher, 2001). Feminist education continues to be marginal to and consciously critical of traditional educational approaches in the academy. At the same time, feminist education has developed a niche within universities that, in some contexts, enjoys institutional legitimacy.

The nature of the women's movement and the early women's studies programs in the academy also promoted interdisciplinary work (Cohee et al., 1998). Early feminist educators worked across, at some professional risk, what had been constructed as impermeable disciplinary borders. Although they themselves were frequently trained within narrow disciplinary boundaries, feminist teachers, using the heuristic of women's oppression as a guiding force, drew attention to common themes and concepts in different academic disciplines. They frequently used constructs from one discipline to uncover sexist practices within another. For example, principles from economics demonstrate the unstated costs of child rearing that have principally been borne by women. Similarly, feminist scholars often banded together for intellectual support and challenge in interdisciplinary feminist enclaves, many of which could be considered informal women's studies groups.

In today's academy, with the acceptance of feminist approaches to scholarly work in many scholarly outlets, feminist faculty can peruse an assortment of discipline-specific feminist literature in the top journals in their fields. Many feminist educators find collegial acceptance within their home departments, eliminating the necessity to look to feminists in other disciplines for intellectual stimulation and encouragement, a situation that can be seen as both a luxury and a potential liability. Without continuing impetus to traverse interdisciplinary boundaries, feminists risk creating the same isolated knowledge silos of which they were once so adamantly critical. Further, they risk reifying disciplinary boundaries that limit the questions posed about gendered relations and equity.

Feminist education continually reexamines the question of epistemology, what we know and how we know it. In particular, feminist educators ask, Do current constructions of knowledge and the methods that produce it systematically oppress women (and other marginalized groups) and, if so, how? (Kramarae & Spender, 1992). Feminist educators problematize what we know, how we know it, and how we teach it. As such, feminist education is constantly changing, questioning, and reforming based on students, the field of study, the sociopolitical climate, and the faculty member her- or himself. It interrogates all aspects of the learning environment, from the institutional context to the authority of the teacher to the personal experiences of the student.

In addition to this continual flux in feminist education, the recognition and celebration of diversity among women leads feminist educators to be suspicious of a singular, monolithic theoretical orientation. The diverse experiences of oppression faced by women of color, lesbians, and working-class women continue to illustrate how gender-based oppressions can operate in unique ways for different women (Hirsch & Keller, 1990; hooks, 1994). What might be seen as positive for one group of women—for example, the ability to enter into the work force—may be an oppressive feature for others who cannot escape the necessity to work outside their homes. Similarly, within the feminist classroom, educators must continually interrogate how educational practices might help or hurt a given group of students. How do culture, class, race, gender, sexual orientation, and, most importantly, the intersections of these identity characteristics shape the learning experiences of the students and the teacher? This question guides much inquiry about the interactions and outcomes that are present in feminist education.

Civic Education

Like feminist education, civic education resists one static definition (Cogan & Derricott, 2000; Mutch, 2003). In fact, Tobias (2000) asserts, "Notions of democracy, citizenship and citizenship education are controversial: their meanings are grounded in a range of political histories, and they have been shaped by the material conditions characterizing successive epochs and by the discourses to which these have given rise" (p. 419). Still, scholarship in this area generally characterizes civic education as curricular and pedagogical strategies meant to enhance the ability of students to contribute positively to society. These strategies take many shapes, including academic learning, democratic citizenship learning, diversity learning, political learning, inter- and intrapersonal learning, social responsibility learning, and leadership learning (Howard, 2001).

Higher education has a long-standing commitment to the development of civic actors (Bowen, 1977; Rhoads, 1997). In the colonial era, colleges were seen to have a moral dimension that focused on character development as well as loyalty to the nation (Rudolph, 1990). Indeed, some scholars argue that the sole purpose of early colleges and universities was the development of a moral character and intellectual skills in a select group of individuals who would provide social and political leadership for the new republic (Colby & Ehrlich, 2000; Giroux, 1983). The rise of a scientific approach to the management of education and the commodification of university education as an individualized benefit demoted the civic purposes of higher education to an afterthought weakly attached to the primary focus of training for professional careers. Consumerism associated with college students also contributed to a minimizing of attention to civic education and engagement (Levine & Cureton, 1998).

Currently, however, increased attention is being given to the need for colleges and universities to help students develop as civic actors. Scholarship in civic education generally focuses on students' abilities to develop skills, knowledge, and motivation that would lead to their "understanding of ethical and social issues, consideration of multiple perspectives on these issues, willingness to take responsibility for their own actions, commitment to contribute to society, and appreciation of cultural pluralism and global interdependence" (Colby, Ehrlich, Beaumont, & Stephens, 2003, p. 52). With regard to specific learning outcomes, civic education should help students develop "critical and integrative thinking, communication, and problem solving, self-understanding of self-knowledge in relation to community, awareness of and willingness to take responsibility for one's actions, informed and responsible involvement, pluralism and cultural awareness and respect, and appreciation of the global dimensions of issues" (Colby et al., p. 53). This definition supports Cogan's (2000a) assertion that citizenship generally addresses five aspects: a sense of identity, the enjoyment of certain rights, the fulfillment of corresponding obligations, a degree of interest and involvement in public affairs, and an acceptance of basic societal values.

Scholars interested in supporting civic education in colleges and universities pose important questions for crafting educational practices. To what extent and in what ways do people in higher education have a responsibility to serve their communities directly—for example, through service-learning and community-based initiatives—rather than indirectly through the "detached" education of students? To what extent and in what ways should civic education incorporate moral and political dimensions, as well as help students develop skills and abilities for living in community with others? How do diversity and international perspectives inform civic education?

Complementary Values and Strategies

As is clear from the foregoing discussion, there are points of agreement in the scholarly tenets associated with feminist education and civic education. In this section, we turn to overlapping values. A key agreement between feminist and civic educators is the belief that values are inherent in educational processes and that it is important to be explicit about those values. As such, we review common values between these two scholarly approaches, focusing on (1) learning through engagement, (2) power/empowerment, and (3) communities. While situating our arguments in terms of values, we associate those values with particular strategies emerging from or advocated by feminist and civic educators.

Learning Through Engagement

Educators who promote feminist and civic approaches to postsecondary education value the engagement of university students in a variety of experiences, both traditional and nontraditional. Engagement centers on understanding relevant knowledge (through the use of both traditional and nontraditional sources) and, subsequently, examining that knowledge in light of students' experience. Many feminist and civic educators incorporate experiential learning and active reflection into their efforts to engage students. In both traditions, faculty's historical role as the sole source of knowledge in the classroom is unraveled.

Feminist education. As mentioned previously, early feminist educators drew directly from consciousness-raising practices in the women's movement as they developed a distinctly feminist pedagogy. Feminist educators, to a greater or lesser extent, draw on students' lived experience of oppression when constructing knowledge in the classroom. In contrast to traditional approaches, in which knowledge is presented in abstract forms and only later, frequently as an afterthought, connected to applications in the "real world," feminist pedagogies frequently begin with students' personal experiences, develop knowledge from those experiences, and then compare that knowledge to existing texts, norms, and practices. The similarities and differences among the multiple knowledge sources that are considered form the basis for scholarly examination.

In feminist education, students and faculty jointly construct knowledge in a process that blends the lived experiences of all participants in the learning community with feminist theory. As bell hooks (1994) states, "When our lived experience of theorizing is fundamentally linked to processes of self-recovery, of collective liberation, no gap exists between theory and practice. Indeed, what such experience makes more evident is the bond between the two—that ultimately reciprocal process wherein one enables the other" (p. 61). The instructional techniques utilized by feminist educators may, at first glance, resemble traditional lecture or discussion methods. The acknowledgment of personal experience as a primary means for constructing knowledge, however, sets feminist educational practices apart from more conventional instructional approaches.

Civic education. Civic educators value educational engagement as a means to learn about others, as well as about how to be deliberate actors working to improve one's community or participate in one's governmental structure. This engagement can come through in-class reflection on the way one's own experiences affect or are affected by engagement with the educational material presented. At the same time, engagement can come through out-of-class interactions with others through the use of service learning or community service (Eyler & Giles, 1999). These opportunities for student engagement with multiple others lead to a better understanding of the broad sociopolitical context about which civic actions must be informed.

One example of civic education is service learning. In service learning, the authoritative role of the faculty member is transformed to a role of facilitator and resource. Simultaneously, community partners take an expanded role as knowledge producers and disseminators. Students, through their service commitments, temporarily take on the role of expert in providing some specific knowledge or skill to the individuals at their service site. In these ways, then, students in the civic education learning environment are more engaged and less passive than students in traditional classrooms.

Parallels and contrasts. Feminist and civic educators offer different rationales and critiques for students' engagement. Yet the underlying assertion that engagement that goes beyond traditional in-class methods is crucial to student learning is a commonly held value. As such, feminist and civic educators often use teaching and learning strategies that emphasize service learning, community involvement, knowledge of and engagement with various groups in the larger community, and an examination of the moral and political implications of education.

Literature and practices associated with feminist education and civic education are not identical, however. Instead, they emphasize different aspects of engagement and consider those aspects in relation to their implications for student learning and educational outcomes. First, civic education often sets up experiences to ensure that students gain experiential knowledge that can then enhance their knowledge of a given course topic. Although feminist education also sets up opportunities for experiential learning, it differs in that it assumes that students come to their learning experiences with knowledge based on previous social interactions. In both cases, the interactions serve as a legitimate knowledge source that may or may not need to be supplemented by other out-of-class engagements.

In addition, civic education assumes that to be a civic actor, associated skills must be learned. Feminist education suggests that although critical approaches to living and understanding can certainly be fostered, students already have the capability to be critical actors in their own lives, and that this agency can be extrapolated to action on behalf of entire communities.

Finally, feminist education often focuses on the past, learning from history about oppressive relationships, policies, and institutions. Civic education tends to focus on the future, using history deliberately to inform current and potential future practices.

Power/Empowerment

Power and empowerment are also key values in both feminist and civic education, although they often have different foci. In both traditions, the conventional authority structures of the classroom, best illustrated through Freire's (1990) "banking model of education," are realigned. Teachers in both civic education and feminist education possess both pedagogical and content-area expertise in their disciplines, but the focus of the classroom is on the collaborative social construction of meaning and the application of those meanings to the lives of the students and others in the broader community. Both approaches to education suggest that a key value of education is to help people develop their own abilities to act in the world in thoughtful ways.

Feminist education. Feminist educators, with the phrase "the personal is political," seek to unmask hegemonic forces that oppress individuals through gendered, raced, and classed expectations. Their own teaching practices are designed to empower students in many ways. As Bee (1993) writes,

> Teaching women to read and write through critical analysis of generative themes which reflect their lives and experience will not of itself bring about a "revolution" in attitudes toward women and the manner in which they are treated. Hopefully, however, it will enable women to travel with a different consciousness of their world, their place within it, and their personal and collective power to transform what is inhumane and unjust within their current circumstances. (p. 107)

Empowerment does not happen in the same ways for all students, nor does a feminist teacher dictate the manner of empowerment. Yet feminist education attempts to help students develop an informed stance on which they can rely when taking action to improve one's own situation or some aspect of the larger community.

The focus on personal experience as a road to understanding and insight is complementary to the feminist perspective on agency. A primary purpose of all feminist education is to draw attention to oppression and, by uncovering its origins and causes, to provide avenues for ending it. Feminist education recognizes that we are all social actors who are capable of contributing to a collective understanding of oppression.

In addition to empowering students to act outside the classroom, feminist educators, especially those coming from radical or poststructural perspectives, such as Ellsworth (1992), Gore (1993), and Orner (1992), look more closely at the question of classroom authority, asking, What types of power should teachers and students have? What should the outcomes of those power enactments in education be? In the feminist classroom, students are encouraged to interrogate the often unquestioned authority of the teacher and to participate in the construction of their individual and collective learning experiences. Power and empowerment are problematized, as it is not always obvious how they influence either learning or community agency.

Civic education. In the civic education movement, specifically with the pedagogy of service learning, community partners, faculty, and students have an interdependent and reciprocal relationship. As Cogan (2000b) states, "We need to begin with the restructuring of the school as we currently know it into one that is a model community of the concept and practice of multidimensional citizenship. This is fundamental" (p. 200). Specifically, civic education stresses the ways in which students can learn to be civic actors by developing skills, knowledge, and motivation (Colby et al., 2003). As Colby and her colleagues assert,

> We believe that a morally and civically responsible individual recognizes himself or herself as a member of a larger social fabric and therefore considers social problems to be at least partly his or her own; such an individual is willing to see the moral and civic dimensions of issues, to make and justify informed moral and civic judgments, and to take action when appropriate. (p. 17)

Action based on one's position as a member of a larger community (whether that be a local, national, or global one) is an important consideration in civic education. Of course, how people conceive of their community influences how they participate in the teaching and learning associated with civic education. For example, some people suggest that civic education should be institutionalized in such a way that students experience a comprehensive education focused on moral and civic issues. Others construct civic education as more directly related to political or governmental structures (Colby et al., 2003). Regardless of the community or one's implementation of particular strategies, however, civic education assumes that students will take a part in constructing that community and helping to improve it in whatever way that is defined.

Parallels and contrasts. In both traditions, empowerment is simultaneously paired with the expectation of responsibility. In Barber's (2001) discussion of the necessity of learning how to function in democratic environments, he writes, "Because we regard ourselves as born free, we take our liberty for granted. We assume that our freedom can be enjoyed without responsibility and that, like some great perpetual motion machine, our democracy can run forever without the fuel of civic activity by engaged citizens" (p. 11). Both feminist and civic educators recognize the need to promote actively not only the learning associated with empowerment but also the responsibility that accompanies that empowerment.

As in the case of engagement, literature and practices associated with feminist and civic education are not identical when considering power and empowerment. First, although feminist education recognizes the need to combine knowledge and action, it does not necessarily consider how that combination can be achieved as students begin to engage with societal structures (including those related to organizations in the local community, as well as those specifically related to government). Perhaps because of civic education's explicit future orientation (students are expected to make communities "better places"), the skills-based elements of civic education facilitate practical knowledge about how to engage in current political systems.

Second, unlike feminist education, civic education does not necessarily consider the effects of gender and other identity characteristics on civic participation. In other words, it does not always consider the ways in which different "civic actors," using the same skills and approaches, may have different access to existing civic and community structures.

Third, feminist education critiques power relations that exist not only in the broader society but also in the classroom. Civic education does not necessarily problematize those power relations, often relying on the faculty member to guide students' educational experiences.

Finally, the public/private dichotomy is often maintained as civic educators emphasize how to engage effectively as a public actor. Feminist education often refers to an oft-used phrase in the feminist movement: The personal is political. In other words, private and public are intertwined, both affecting the other in meaningful ways. This belief is incorporated into feminist education in efforts to empower, using knowledge gained through personal and public experiences as a base. In these ways, feminist and civic education define political involvement differently, each emphasizing a particular way of conceptualizing what it means to be empowered to participate in political processes and change efforts.

Communities

Both feminist and civic education stress the importance of thinking of individuals and social institutions in the context of the various communities in which they are situated. Both traditions focus on community, emphasizing that identities matter in and out of education, and assert that education and society are interrelated. This community orientation takes shape in classroom environments in a variety of ways in feminist and civic education.

Feminist education. People involved in feminist education believe that one's identification with various communities—because of the experiences one might have through those communities—is particularly important for developing knowledge, educational practices, and orientations. As Sánchez-Casal and Macdonald (2002) write, "We therefore recommend that feminists continue to ground our teaching on the claim that there are real social, political, and epistemic consequences of identity, but that we reject essentialist feminist and liberation theories that understand identity to be fully determinate of what and how we know" (p. 3). Although both approaches to education consider that participants are involved in a variety of communities, and that their educational experiences should help them develop the ability to function in a wide range of settings, feminist educators suggest that the overlapping nature of communities is sometimes problematic, in that communities (associated with identity or social roles, for example) can actually contradict and work against one another (Adair & Dahlberg, 2003; Rockhill, 1993).

Civic education. Education clearly plays a key role in students' development as members of multiple communities. Recently, advocates of citizenship education encourage an education that crosses boundaries associated with those communities. Kubow, Grossman, and Ninomiya (2000) assert,

> Multidimensional citizenship would require that we provide a deliberative and reflective framework for students to understand their multiple roles at all levels and provide them with the skills to cross boundaries, whether they be geographical or cultural. To this end, the concept of education for international understanding and cooperation should be developed and expanded so that students view themselves as members of several overlapping communities. (p. 139)

Civic education can be grounded in local or global knowledge, emphasizing the need to consider both when developing political practices. One's community of origin (which is often integrally tied to one's self-understanding and identity) and one's current community are both important to understanding how students learn and how that learning affects subsequent involvement in those communities.

Parallels and contrasts. Both feminist and civic education traditions arrange classroom experiences to ensure that students develop the skills necessary to negotiate the contradictions inherent in membership in multiple communities. Both traditions help students to analyze critically the roles that they wish to play in the larger society.

As is clear from the foregoing discussion, though, the two traditions also differ in their approaches to the concept of community. Civic education emphasizes one's engagement in a larger society, but it does so in a way that does not necessarily foreground the salience of gender and other identities as they affect one's ability to become civically engaged. Much of the civic education literature presupposes a type of grand narrative for community engagement, emphasizing the development of skills and motivation for involvement. Feminist education, on the other hand, continually uses the construct of gender (as well as of race, ethnicity, sexual orientation, and socioeconomic status) to help students interrogate unquestioned community structures and practices. For example, students and educators in feminist classrooms may ask, Who is in charge of particular governmental or community structures? Are all potential participants equally empowered to participate in communities that, by definition, include them? By foregrounding various oppressive practices, feminist educators enable students to respond critically and intentionally to their sometimes shifting roles within various socially constructed communities.

Also, feminist education frequently takes on an almost utopian vision of the potential of community. Disillusioned with current and past patriarchal structures, feminism looks toward a future absent of oppression. Within civic education, however, there is a splintered view of community. As Peters and Marshall (1996) write, "Where the radical view [of civic education] looks to the future to establish true community, the conservative view locates community in the cherished past" (p. 25). As such, there exists a further tension between feminist education—which is explicitly change oriented in an attempt to minimize oppression—and a conservative type of civic education, which seeks to restore previously established communities that may benefit members of those communities differentially.

Other Tensions Among the Discourses Associated with Civic Education and Feminist Education

The preceding discussion has emphasized the three values of learning through engagement, power/empowerment, and community within civic education and feminist education, but other important tensions between the two discourses go beyond these three values. For example, the two educational movements have quite different historical and current relationships to the "mainstream" structures of higher education in the United States. As mentioned earlier, the academy has traditionally accepted the idea of a civic focus to higher education, even though it has at times not acted on that concept. Feminist education, however, began outside the mainstream of higher education and has remained, to some extent, critical of it. Whereas feminist educators often, though not exclusively, are found among the ranks of junior faculty, civic education is frequently espoused by both junior and senior faculty and senior administrators within institutions, the most noticeable evidence being the visibility of college presidents as leaders within the Campus Compact organization. Over time, feminist educators have expressed some hesitancy to become legitimized by the academy because of the dangers of feminist work being "corrupted" by the very academic structures that support it (Frye, 1983; hooks, 1994). In contrast, civic educators actively seek to be institutionalized in higher education and to expand their role in transforming the stated and enacted missions of higher education institutions (Colby et al., 2003; Furco, 2001).

Implications for Policy and Practice

With the increasing commodification of higher education, both feminist and civic education progressively appear as somewhat radical philosophies of education. Both discourses eschew a model of student as merely consumer, emphasizing instead a need for community involvement and participation in deliberate social change. As such, they are both critical of current administrative practices that construct students as isolated individuals who "buy" educational products from the college or university that assembles the best marketing strategy. Instead, both civic and feminist education discourses construct students as active participants who are informed by and can, in turn, actively inform their communities.

Both traditions seek to engage students actively in learning that is transformed by and transforms the world outside the academy. Both traditions problematize a view of faculty as factory workers who pour static discipline-specific knowledge into the empty vessels of students as they march along a production line of educational lectures and labs. In this way, both feminist and civic education can serve as a counterbalance to current discourses that frame higher education institutions as businesses (Roberts, 1998) and advocate policies that oversimplify the educational process and dehumanize students, faculty, and staff.

These two educational communities might also strengthen their own discourses and instructional practices by examining their similarities and differences. For example, civic education may become more relevant to the increasingly diverse college-student population if it were to examine closely feminist education's deconstruction of multiple, overlapping identities. Civic education could greatly benefit from a critical focus on the ways in which varied identities affect access to and involvement in civic structures.

Similarly, feminist education, while valuing empowerment and agency, does little specifically to build community-engagement skills among students. Students in feminist classrooms may be inspired to community activism, but they may frequently lack direction in how to accomplish their activist goals effectively. Feminist educators could benefit from the model of civic education that helps students to participate actively in community engagement through service learning or other community-based pedagogies.

Significance

> The struggle of diverse students to instill a broader realization of American democracy brings to mind one of the central obligations embraced by student development and the traditions of liberal learning: Education for citizenship is a key aspect of the college student experience. (Rhoads, 1997, p. 51)

The significance of this analysis is manifold. First, it contributes to higher education scholars' understandings of both feminist education and civic education by disentangling the similarities and differences of these scholarly traditions. Second, currently much of the scholarship related to both feminist and civic education derives from K–12 literature. This chapter brings the dialogue more concretely to bear on higher education settings. Third, this chapter suggests an ability for each of these discourses to be strengthened by the other, an especially important task given the threats to higher education from neoliberal, consumer-oriented education that values students primarily as future consumers, rather than as engaged and empowered citizens (Peters &

Roberts, 1999). Finally, the chapter demonstrates how both of these approaches to education have the potential to strengthen the role of higher education in fostering communities in education and in other social institutions. In an era when the diverse participation of both scholars and students is a national and global imperative, civic and feminist education hold great promise.

References

Adair, V. C., & Dahlberg, S. L. (2003). *Reclaiming class: Women, poverty, and the promise of higher education in America.* Philadelphia: Temple University Press.

Barber, B. (2001). An aristocracy of everyone. In S. J. Goodlad (Ed.), *The last best hope: A democracy reader* (pp. 11–22). San Francisco: Jossey-Bass.

Bee, B. (1993). Critical literacy and the politics of gender. In C. Lankshear & P. L. McLaren (Eds.), *Critical literacy: Politics, praxis, and the postmodern* (pp. 105–131). Albany: State University of New York Press.

Bowen, H. R. (1977). *Investment in learning.* San Francisco: Jossey-Bass.

Cogan, J. J. (2000a). Citizenship education for the 21st century: Setting the context. In J. J. Cogan & R. Derricott (Eds.), *Citizenship for the 21st century: An international perspective on education* (pp. 1–21). London: Kogan Page.

Cogan, J. J. (2000b). The challenge of multidimensional citizenship for the 21st century. In J. J. Cogan & R. Derricott (Eds.), *Citizenship for the 21st century: An international perspective on education* (pp. 189–201). London: Kogan Page.

Cogan, J. J., & Derricott, R. (2000). *Citizenship for the 21st century: An international perspective on education.* London: Kogan Page.

Cohee, G. E., Daumer, E., Kemp, T. D., Krebs, P., Lafky, S., & Runzo, S. (1998). Collectively speaking. In G. E. Cohee, E. Daumer, T. Kemp, P. Krebs, S. Lafky, & S. Runzo (Eds.), *The feminist teacher anthology: Pedagogies and classroom strategies* (pp. 1–10). New York: Teachers College Press.

Colby, A., & Ehrlich, T. (2000). Higher education and the development of civic responsibility. In T. Ehrlich (Ed.), *Civic responsibility and higher education* (pp. xxi–xliii). Westport, CT: Oryx Press.

Colby, A., Ehrlich, T., Beaumont, E., & Stephens, J. (2003). *Educating citizens: Preparing America's undergraduates for lives of moral and civic responsibility.* San Francisco: Jossey-Bass.

Ellsworth, E. (1992). Why doesn't this feel empowering? Working through the repressive myths of critical pedagogy. In C. Luke & J. Gore (Eds.), *Feminism and critical pedagogy* (pp. 90–119). New York: Routledge.

Eyler, J., & Giles, D. (1999). *Where's the learning in service-learning?* San Francisco: Jossey-Bass.

Fisher, B. M. (2001). *No angel in the classroom: Teaching through feminist discourse.* Lanham, MD: Rowman & Littlefield.

Freire, P. (1990). *Pedagogy of the oppressed.* New York: Continuum.

Frye, M. (1983). *The politics of reality: Essays in feminist theory.* Freedom, CA: Crossing Press.

Furco, A. (2001). Advancing service-learning at research universities. In M. Canada & B. Speck (Eds.), *New Directions for Higher Education No. 114: Developing and implementing service-learning programs* (pp. 67–78). San Francisco: Jossey-Bass.

Giroux, H. (1983). Critical theory and rationality in citizenship education. In H. Giroux & D. Purpel (Eds.), *The hidden curriculum and moral education.* Berkeley, CA: McCutchan.

Gore, J. (1993). *The struggle for pedagogies: Critical and feminist discourses as regimes of truth.* New York: Routledge.

Hirsch, M., & Keller, E. F. (1990). *Conflicts in feminism.* New York: Routledge.

hooks, b. (1994). *Teaching to transgress: Education as the practice of freedom.* New York: Routledge.

Howard, J. (2001, fall). Service learning course design workbook [Special issue]. *Michigan Journal of Community Service Learning.*

Kramarae, C., & Spender, D. (1992). *The knowledge explosion: Generations of feminist scholarship.* New York: Teachers College Press.

Kubow, P., Grossman, D., & Ninomiya, A. (2000). Multidimensional citizenship: Educational policy for the 21st century. In J. J. Cogan & R. Derricott (Eds.), *Citizenship for the 21st century: An international perspective on education* (pp. 131–150). London: Kogan Page.

Levine, A., & Cureton, J. S. (1998). *When hope and fear collide: A portrait of today's college student.* San Francisco: Jossey-Bass.

Maher, F. A., & Tetreault, M. K. T. (1994). *The feminist classroom.* New York: Basic Books.

Mutch, C. (2003). *Citizenship education in New Zealand: Inside or outside the curriculum?* Paper presented at the annual meeting of the American Educational Research Association, Chicago, IL.

Orner, M. (1992). Interrupting the calls for student voice in "liberatory" education: A feminist poststructuralist perspective. In C. Luke & J. Gore (Eds.), *Feminism and critical pedagogy* (pp. 74–89). New York: Routledge.

Peters, M., & Marshall, J. (1996). *Individualism and community: Education and social policy in the postmodern condition.* London: Falmer.

Peters, M., & Roberts, P. (1999). *University futures and the politics of reform in New Zealand.* Palmerston North, New Zealand: Dunmore Press.

Rhoads, R. A. (1997). Interpreting identity politics: The educational challenge of contemporary student activism. *Journal of College Student Development, 38*(5), 508–519.

Roberts, P. (1998), Scholarly life in virtual universities. In M. Peters & P. Roberts (Eds.), *Virtual universities and tertiary education* (pp. 111–133). Palmerston North, New Zealand: Dunmore Press.

Rockhill, K. (1993). (Dis)connecting literacy and sexuality: Speaking the unspeakable in the classroom. In C. Lankshear & P. L. McLaren (Eds.), *Critical literacy: Politics, praxis, and the postmodern* (pp. 335–366). Albany: State University of New York Press.

Ropers-Huilman, B. (1998). *Feminist teaching in theory and practice: Situating power and knowledge in poststructural classrooms.* New York: Teachers College Press.

Ropers-Huilman, B. (2002). Feminist education. In K. Kinser & J. Forest (Eds.), *Encyclopedia of higher education* (pp. 254–258). Santa Barbara, CA: ABC-CLIO.

Rudolph, F. (1990). *The American college and university: A history.* Athens: University of Georgia Press.

Sánchez-Casal, S., & Macdonald, A. A. (2002). Feminist reflections on the pedagogical relevance of identity. In A. A. Macdonald & S. Sánchez-Casal (Eds.), *Twenty-first century feminist classrooms* (pp. 1–30). New York: Palgrave Macmillan.

Shor, I. (1993). Education is politics: Paulo Freire's critical pedagogy. In P. McLaren & P. Leonard (Eds.), *Paulo Freire: A critical encounter* (pp. 25–35). New York: Routledge.

Tobias, R. (2000). The boundaries of adult education for active citizenship—institutional and community contexts. *International Journal of Lifelong Education, 19*(5), 418–429.

2

LEARNING PARTNERSHIPS

A Gender-Inclusive Model for Undergraduate Teaching

Marcia B. Baxter Magolda

I wish teachers wouldn't do so many multiple-choice questions and have some more thinking type things because life is not multiple choice. I've been realizing out here, I mean, there's so many things I have to think about and look up and research and think about more. It seems like in college and high school everything is just so multiple choice, "Memorize this and spit it out." And that's mostly all I ever did, memorize, memorize, memorize, and learn facts and just spit it out to someone and circle answers and that was it. I wish we'd done—I don't know—more thinking things or stuff like that.

—Anne (Baxter Magolda, 2001, p. 193)

Anne, a participant in my longitudinal study of young adults' learning and development (Baxter Magolda, 1992, 2001), uses the phrase "out here" to refer to her first postcollege job in accounting. Her experience of memorizing in college fell short of preparing her to think about her work, search for relevant information and evidence, and make decisions about how to proceed. Anne's reflection supports the vision of 21st-century higher education advocated in numerous national reform reports. For example, the authors of *Greater Expectations: A New Vision for Learning as a Nation Goes to College* (Association of American Colleges and Universities, 2002) advocate educating students to become intentional learners:

In a turbulent and complex world, every college student will need to be purposeful and self-directed in multiple ways. . . . Intentional learners are integrative thinkers who can see connections in seemingly disparate information and draw on a wide range of knowledge to make decisions. They adapt the skills learned in one situation to problems encountered in another: in a classroom, the workplace, their communities, or their personal lives. As a result, intentional learners succeed even when instability is the only constant. (pp. 21–22)

The need to be self-directed in a complex world, however, does not mean being self-centered, as is evident in *Greater Expectations*:

For intentional learners, intellectual study connects to personal life, formal education to work, and knowledge to social responsibility. Through understanding the power and implications of education, learners who are intentional consciously choose to act in ethical and responsible ways. Able to place themselves in the context of a diverse world, these learners draw on difference and commonality to produce a deeper experience of community. (p. 22)

Intentional learners combine responsibility for personal actions and civic values. Success in adult life and responsible citizenship thus require both individual and communal capability. A successful adult requires cognitive maturity to analyze and coordinate information to make wise decisions, personal maturity to clarify one's goals and intentions, and relational maturity to engage in mutual collaboration with diverse others.

Cognitive, personal, and relational maturity entail far more than skills in these respective areas. They require self-authorship—the capacity to define internally a coherent belief system and identity that coordinates mutual relations with others (Baxter Magolda, 2004b; Kegan, 1994). Internally defining a coherent belief system hinges on viewing knowledge as contextual and viewing oneself as capable of making knowledge claims based on relevant evidence. Internally defining a coherent identity necessitates the capacity to choose values and organize them to regulate choices. Defining an internal belief system and identity contributes to the capacity to engage in authentic, interdependent relationships with diverse others. Self-authorship is the developmental capacity that underlies many of the expectations that college graduates like Anne face in adult life. The collective experience of my longitudinal participants revealed that they were socialized in college to depend on authorities and struggled to meet the expectation to be self-authored in postcollege life (Baxter Magolda, 2001). These data and the key emphasis of most national reform reports suggest that helping college students move from authority dependence to self-authorship is a necessity for success in adult life and thus ought to be the primary goal of higher education.

Self-Authorship as a Blend of Connection and Autonomy

Connection, a central feature of theories of women's development (e.g., Belenky, Clinchy, Goldberger, & Tarule, 1986; Gilligan, 1982; Josselson, 1996), refers to the ability to link with others and function in collaborative ways. Autonomy, a central feature of theories of men's development (e.g., Chickering, 1969; Kohlberg, 1984; Perry, 1970), refers to separating from others to function as an autonomous individual. Contemporary adult development research indicates that these two concepts are combined in complex development (Baxter Magolda, 2001; Jordan, 2004; Kegan, 1994). Self-authorship does not connote the historical emphasis on the individuating, agentic self; instead it reflects an authentic self that is capable of genuine connection to others and the world. Mutuality can be defined as possible when each person is able to "represent her or his own experience in a relationship, to act in a way which is congruent with an 'inner truth' and with the context, and to respond to and encourage authenticity in the other person" (Miller et al., pp. 25–49). For my longitudinal participants, defining this inner truth involved gradually extracting themselves from uncritical dependence on external authority to learn to analyze their experience, decide what to believe, and choose values to guide their lives. Clarity about their belief system and values enhanced their capacity for mutual empathy, connection building, and empowering others—skills that Jordan (2004) identifies as central to relational competence. Thus, internally coordinating one's belief system, values, and interdependent relations with others requires a complex blend of connection and autonomy.

Longitudinal participants' stories illustrate this complex blend of connection and autonomy, as well as the necessity for self-authorship in adult life. For example, Lydia is raising two small children while her husband's Navy ship is deployed to the other side of the world. Talking about how she was handling these circumstances, she said,

> I'd like to think that I'm taking the uncertainty in stride. We'd been given a return date for my husband's ship in September—then found out it

would be another four weeks after that date. You just have to roll with it. Getting angry just takes a lot of energy that you can't expend on something you can't control or change. Things I can control, I do—things I can't, just let go. I don't want people to have pity on me—others have more difficult situations than I have. Think about those people who died in the World Trade Center—all those people who are left. My husband is e-mailing me daily, he loves me, he'll be back. Millions of people have more difficult situations than I do. That is how I choose to look at it. This is a temporary bump in the road of life. I know that is helping me get through every day and every moment best I can. I've learned to say "that is the best I can do right now." There are limitations sometimes—so be it.

Lydia's ability to shape her interpretation of external events over which she has no control (e.g., "That is how I choose to look at it") stems from the internal belief system and identity that she constructed over the course of her twenties. She exhibits self-confidence to handle this situation and awareness of her own limitations. Her interdependent relationship with her husband yields empathy for his being in a dangerous setting without access to his family rather than frustration about her own challenge of raising two small boys with no help. She empathizes with others whom she does not even know personally. Her self-authorship, evident in her connection to her authentic self and to the needs of others, helps her function autonomously in less-than-ideal circumstances.

Learning Partnerships: Blending Connection and Autonomy

The self-authorship illustrated in the lives of the longitudinal participants revealed that connection and autonomy are both necessary for maturity. Participants' journey toward self-authorship yielded gender-related patterns with varying emphasis on connection and autonomy. In this chapter I use women's narratives to trace how connection and autonomy evolved for my participants from age 18 to 36. I also offer a gender-inclusive pedagogical model to promote self-authorship. This Learning Partnerships Model (Baxter Magolda, 2004a), which grew out of participants' collective experience, invites learners to bring their own experience and identity into a mutual learning relationship. As such, it welcomes both connected and autonomous pattern learners and assists both in blending connection and autonomy so that they can internally construct belief systems, identities, and mutual relationships. Welcoming both patterns is particularly important in light of evidence that higher education typically emphasizes autonomy over connection, thus limiting students' ability to achieve the mature blend of the two concepts needed for self-authorship.

A Gendered Journey Toward Self-Authorship

Questions about the role of gender in learning and development prompted me to initiate a longitudinal study in 1986 with 101 entering college students (51 women and 50 men). Eighty of these students participated in an annual interview during all four years of their college experience. The interview focused on their assumptions about the nature of knowledge; the role of the learner, instructor, peers, and evaluation in learning; and the nature of their decision making. The 432 interviews that I conducted with these students over the first five years of the study yielded four sets of assumptions about knowledge that ranged from viewing knowledge as absolute to viewing it as contextual (Baxter Magolda, 1992). Two distinct but equally complex gender-related patterns—one emphasizing autonomy and one emphasizing connection—were evident in these sets of assumptions and merged in viewing knowledge as contextual. These data confirmed that what Belenky et al. (1986) labeled separate and connected approaches to knowing were equally complex and that both approaches were required in complex forms of knowing.

Following 70 participants into their postcollege years broadened the scope of the study to include a more balanced focus on assumptions about knowledge (the epistemological dimension), self (the intrapersonal dimension), and relationships (the interpersonal dimension). The nearly 500 additional interviews conducted in the last 15 years of the study demonstrate how these three dimensions are intertwined in the journey toward self-authorship. In the following section, I trace this journey as a foundation for the Learning Partnerships Model's utility in promoting self-authorship during college. Despite the inclusion of men in the study, I use women's narratives to emphasize that women vary in their socialization toward connection and autonomy.

Following External Formulas

Participants began—and many left—college relying on external formulas provided by authority figures for their beliefs, identities, and relationships. As an entering student, Bev reported her approach to learning:

When the teacher lectures, I take notes and try to understand what he says. I have a teacher right now who won't quit zipping out facts, and it's really hard for me to get them all down. Sometimes, I focus in on more of what he's saying, and I can go back and find the facts myself. I try to understand just the important points. I am trying to take down both facts and concepts. But if I have trouble because the teacher is going too fast, I try to concentrate more on what they are trying to get at. That's the important part of the lecture. (Baxter Magolda, 1992, pp. 82–83)

Bev's comments reflect *absolute knowing*, which is characterized by the assumptions that knowledge is certain and that her role is to acquire it from the authority. Focusing on taking in information, she adopted a *receiving pattern* for learning. Marge, another entering student, took a different approach to absolute knowing. She shared, "I like classes where people get involved, where people are talking back and throwing things at you that make you think a little bit harder. It does help to have people around you. Basically, just ask questions and raise them in my mind" (Baxter Magolda, 1992, p. 98). Emphasizing being challenged to think in order to master the material, Marge used the *mastery pattern* to learn. Although Marge's more autonomous approach has traditionally been more valued in the college classroom, both women share the same set of epistemological assumptions. Of the longitudinal participants, 68% used the absolute way of knowing during their first year of college. The receiving pattern, with its emphasis on connection, was more prevalent among the women in the study, whereas the mastery pattern, with its emphasis on autonomy, was more prevalent among the men. I call these *gender-related* patterns because they were not gender exclusive.

College experiences challenged the assumption that knowledge is certain and thus led many students to adopt *transitional knowing*, in which they endorsed knowledge as certain in some areas (e.g., mathematics, science, religion) and uncertain in others (e.g., humanities). Cherylyn illustrated this perspective:

You can disagree in psychology, like in evolution. You can't really disagree with Spanish or zoology. But in psychology, we studied evolution. I'm a Christian and I don't agree with evolution. I just look at the two, try to see what makes sense, what's reasonable, and why I feel a certain way or why I don't. Think of the exceptions, think about situations in my own life and how things have happened there—what I've found to be true in my own experiences. And then what support other people may have. (Baxter Magolda, 1992, p. 115)

Cherylyn's approach to the uncertain areas demonstrates the *interpersonal pattern* within transitional knowing. She connects to her own experience as well as to others' ideas to figure out what to believe. Holly uses an *impersonal pattern* for the same purpose, explaining how she decided what to believe in the face of uncertainty:

Just the fact that you are thinking about it, rather than taking notes and memorizing things. I guess hearing what other people have to say—and then, if you're called on to respond, you have to do some thinking. You definitely learn more if you're thinking about what you're learning rather than just rote memory. (Baxter Magolda, 1992, p. 127)

Holly's focus is not on listening to others' ideas but rather on using their ideas to spark her own thinking. This separate emphasis was more prevalent among men in the study, whereas the connected emphasis was more prevalent among women in the study. Transitional knowing emerged as the predominant way of knowing for sophomores (53%), juniors (83%), and seniors (80%) in this study.

Graduating from college using transitional knowing resulted in many graduates *following external formulas* for success in their professional and private lives. Amy shared how this played out in her graduate school classes:

That's one of my problems I have with writing things, you know, writing papers is actually showing my own ideas. I'm kind of scared of being completely off, and so I think I play the line very straight and I don't really take a lot of chances. And that's one thing I think I worked on in papers, trying to give my own opinion and not feeling that that was going to be completely off. . . . giving my own opinion or something, I'm always worried that what I say is not right. So I think—I know I'm always scared kind of about my creativity I guess, about how when something's in front of me and I have complete rein to do whatever I want, whether it's in a paper or doing a project or doing something, that kind of scares me because I feel like I can do better when I have specific guidelines. You know, "You do this. You answer certain questions," rather than—I don't know—"Here, you have a paper and you can write it on anything you want." And then

I'm just like, "Ooh." I'd rather have a specific question to answer and work it out. (Baxter Magolda, 2001, pp. 86–87)

Amy's hesitation in crafting her own opinions was due in part to holding on to the epistemological assumption that there was a "right" answer. Thus, she questioned her ability to construct a reasonable perspective. However, her comments reveal that her hesitation was also linked to her lack of an internal sense of self to overcome fear of others' reactions. Her reliance on external authority in the epistemological realm extended to the intrapersonal and interpersonal dimensions of her development.

The Crossroads

For a few participants during college and for the majority after college, reliance on the formulas of external authorities came into conflict with the demands of graduate or professional education, employment settings, and community and personal life. Part of this dissonance occurred in the epistemological dimension as experiences prompted participants to adopt *independent knowing* or the assumption that most, if not all, knowledge is uncertain. This uncertainty made it difficult to decide what to believe, as Alexis explained:

> I listen to their arguments for it; then I listen to other people's arguments against it. And then it's just my own personal view, really, whether I can establish the credibility—so I guess it stems from the credibility of the person who's saying it also, as well as just the opinion on it. I listen to both sides. I usually throw some of my own views into it as well. So I'm influenced by other people—like each member of the group should be influenced by each other. But when the final vote comes in, you should go with what you believe. (Baxter Magolda, 1992, pp. 147–148)

I call this approach the *interindividual pattern* because of its focus on connection to others' ideas. Although Alexis advocated using her own personal view and deciding what she believes in the end, she is more accustomed to listening to others than to herself. Valerie, in contrast, emphasized listening to herself as she described her preference for activities that promoted independent thinking:

Case studies, group discussions, learning to interact with other people—I think that really helped you make your own decisions instead of spitting out facts that somebody has told you to memorize. You really make your own decisions, and you think subjectively and objectively about things, and you decide what you want to do and what you think about that. (Baxter Magolda, 1992, p. 159)

Valerie's focus on what she thinks represents the *individual pattern* of independent knowing. This pattern, which emphasizes separation, was prevalent among men in the study, whereas the interindividual pattern, which emphasizes connection, was prevalent among women in the study.

Inherent in independent knowing is the move away from dependence on authority toward the construction of an internal belief system and identity. Although participants were aware of the need to construct beliefs and values to ground themselves when they reframed their relationships with authorities, it was easier said than done. Lauren, involved in a long-distance relationship, articulated what it was like to be in the midst of this *crossroads*:

He came home with me to [my parents' house] and I was totally gung-ho. I'm like, "This is it; I know it." And then after they gave me their feedback, they liked him but they were just not sure. And after they said that, all of a sudden I didn't like him as much anymore. It was nothing that he did to me; it was not the way he acted. It was nothing. But it was because of what they said, all of a sudden I started changing my mind. Yes, that's exactly true. But then my sister, on the other hand, is the opposite and is like, "Just go with how you feel." And my friends, my close friends here are like, "Just go with how you feel." So now it's gotten better. I'm trying to really think of what I want and not what they want. So this relationship is continuing, which they're not upset about at all, but I will tell you they have told me, "Come on, this really isn't going to work. It's too far." And that does affect me. But I'm really trying to take the attitude where maybe I need to find out for myself. But I will admit always in the back of my mind what they think still lingers over my decisions. (Baxter Magolda, 2001, p. 99)

Lauren was aware that she co-constructed her perspective with others whose opinions she trusted more than her own, namely, her parents. Her sister and her friends pulled her in another direction. Lauren knew she needed to find out for herself; she just did not yet have a process for doing so. The crossroads was the phase of the journey toward self-authorship that called on participants, regardless of their gender-related leanings toward connection or autonomy, to find a way to blend the two. Some longitudinal participants found their way through the crossroads by their mid-twenties. Others spent the majority of their twenties, and sometimes their early thirties, working on this challenge.

Self-Authorship

The demand that Anne described at the outset of this chapter—to think, look things up, research, and think more—prompted participants to adopt the assumption that knowledge exists in a context and that beliefs are decided by evaluating relevant evidence. Gwen described this *contextual knowing*:

> As you hear more people's opinions, you piece together what you really think. Who has the valid point? Whose point is not valid in your opinion? And come to some other new understanding from a more dimensional perspective. It's super subjective. A lot of it is weighing people's opinions and their facts against what you yourself have previously processed. I don't care if people feel this way or that way about it. But if they can support their stance and have some background and some backing for that, to my thinking that is valid. (Baxter Magolda, 1992, p. 59)

Contextual knowing blends the previous gender-related patterns. It requires connection to get inside other people's opinions, as well as inside one's own experience and thinking (Gwen's notion of super subjective). Simultaneously it demands autonomy to stand outside one's own and others' experiences and assess the validity of the evidence that each has for his or her stance. Contextual knowing also entails complex assumptions in the intrapersonal and interpersonal dimensions of development. Contextual knowing, as Gwen described, involves judging external perspectives for oneself to "piece together what you really think." Owning responsibility for constructing knowledge in this way necessitates a sense of self that stands apart from others' opinions and judgments—the dilemma that Amy shared earlier in trying to meet the demands of her graduate program. Constructing mutual social relations through which one can gain a multidimensional view without being consumed by others' opinions (as Lauren was struggling with in the cross-roads) is also crucial to contextual knowing.

Maturity on all three dimensions yields self-authorship. Dawn's reflection on coping with multiple sclerosis and its implications for her work and personal life capture her ability to construct beliefs internally, her authentic sense of self, and her ability to connect to herself and others. At 36, she told this story:

> I'm learning a lot about strength coming out of this breakup. . . . It has been a journey into the deepest part of myself. I know me better than I've ever known myself in my life. . . . I know what I want in the big scheme of things, looking for that life partner, someone to share my life with, work together in partnership—created a fairly specific vision for that. Thought this relationship was it, obviously it wasn't for whatever reason. Okay, what do I need to learn about myself in this situation so that I have a better understanding of how to get what I want? . . . When I was diagnosed with MS three years ago, I said, "Okay fine, what do I need to do?" I started riding a bike and stayed very active. When I got into this relationship, I kind of forgot about all of that—focus went to relationship and not me. I started on a downward slide. I went to see my doctor—she said I had gotten worse. That is all I needed to hear. As can happen with this disease, you can go downhill and that's it. From the beginning I've been fine, I understand that I have this disease, but it won't rule my world. Not that Anna (my ex) would ever feel comfortable telling me that was the problem; my intuition is that my not taking care of myself was part of the problem. I was running into stuff, falling down, had no stamina in my legs. I noticed that that was happening, but I was not taking any steps to correct it. It was frustrating me, making me angry. Some of that came out in the relationship—not directed at her—but I stopped approaching myself as someone with a disease that I needed to take care of. I had let go of that. Out of the breakup has come a lot of self-awareness—wow—I really have to take care of myself.

Dawn described connecting to herself to sort out what happened in the relationship. It is from this inner self that she constructed her vision of what she wanted in a partner. When the relationship ended, she explored herself to determine why. In doing so, she reconnected to the importance of managing her disease. She internally constructed her interpretation of her disease, her relationship, and herself. Dawn, Lydia, and other participants who have become self-authored are continuously evolving, yet they have an internal foundation to cope with life's challenges.

Learning Partnerships

In addition to portraying the nature of participants' journey toward self-authorship, my nearly 1,000 longitudinal interviews revealed conditions that enabled participants to achieve the complex blend of connection and autonomy required for the shift from authority dependence to self-authorship. Stories from their undergraduate education, graduate and professional education, employment, and community and personal life contained rich examples of the partnerships that supported this journey. The Learning Partnerships Model (LPM) emerged from synthesizing the key dynamics of these relationships (Baxter Magolda, 2001, 2004a). An observation study of three undergraduate courses, one in zoology, one in mathematics, and a large course on the social foundations of education, further contributed to refining the LPM (Baxter Magolda, 1999). Attending the course sessions, interviewing the instructors, and interviewing the students enrolled (who ranged from entering students to seniors) confirmed that educators could implement in numerous undergraduate contexts the dynamics of learning partnerships described by longitudinal participants. This evidence encouraged a variety of educators to construct learning partnerships in diverse settings. The educators' stories, which include the effects of the LPM on student learning, support the effectiveness of the LPM in an undergraduate writing curriculum, a community college business course, an urban leadership internship program, a cultural immersion program, a community living context, and a graduate program. The LPM has also been used to guide the reorganization of a student affairs division and to shape faculty and curriculum development. These case examples, available in *Learning Partnerships* (Baxter Magolda & King, 2004), affirm that the model is inclusive of a variety of learner characteristics because it engages learners as genuine partners in their education. I present the model and learners' narratives in the following sections and return later to the connection of the LPM to constructivist-developmental and feminist scholarship on learning and pedagogy.

The Learning Partnerships Model

The LPM enables learners to shift from authority dependence to self-authorship by challenging and supporting them to coordinate internally their beliefs, values, and interpersonal loyalties. *Three core assumptions* about learning challenge authority dependence: knowledge is complex and socially constructed, one's identity plays a central role in crafting knowledge claims, and knowledge is mutually constructed via the sharing of expertise and authority. Portraying knowledge as the complex result of experts negotiating what to believe gives learners access to the process of learning and deciding what to believe. Emphasizing that one's identity plays a central role in deciding what to believe enables learners to see their role in knowledge construction. Conceptualizing knowledge as mutually constructed introduces the shared responsibility to engage multiple perspectives to decide what to believe. All three assumptions encourage autonomy through personal responsibility for learning and refining beliefs. They simultaneously encourage connection to one's own and others' perspectives.

Three principles offer the corresponding support to help learners address these challenges: validating learners' capacity as knowledge constructors, situating learning in learners' experience, and defining learning as mutually constructing meaning. Validating learners' capacity to learn and construct knowledge is necessary for them to accept responsibility for internally coordinating their beliefs, values, and interpersonal loyalties. Situating learning in learners' experience invites them to bring their identity to learning. Defining learning as a mutual process of exchanging perspectives to develop knowledge claims supports learners' participation in the social construction of knowledge. The three principles model autonomy (i.e., learners bring their experience and construct their own perspectives) and connection (i.e., learners connect to their own and others' experiences and ideas). This blend of challenge and support provides guidance and empowerment simultaneously, modeling the blend of connection and autonomy inherent in the nature of self-authorship.

Learning Partnerships: Challenging Authority Dependence

Given that many students enter college having been socialized to accept knowledge uncritically, is it possible to challenge authority dependence? A sophomore at Indiana University–Purdue University Indianapolis convinced me that the answer is yes. In her invited response to one of my presentations on learning partnerships, Erin told a story about her most productive learning experience (Hillenburg, 2002). She began by sharing her shock on her first day of college at one of her teachers wearing a sweater that said "Question Authority." Although she questioned whether college would "kill her," she reported that the course eventually changed her outlook on college and learning in general:

> The professor would present thought-provoking information, most of which was new to me. He went about telling the story or giving the facts without drawing conclusions. This gave me the opportunity to come to my own conclusions about the situations that he presented. My entire educational background to that point told me exactly what to think but now I had the opportunity to decide for myself. At first I looked for clues from the professor so I would know the "right" way to think, but he was very good at hiding and disguising his personal beliefs. Because I was not directed by the professor I became eager to find information on my own. I wanted to read the class text and even searched for articles that addressed our topics outside of the classroom. (Baxter Magolda, 2004a, p. 54)

Because Erin's previous education told her what to think, she initially tried to ascertain what her instructor thought was right. His invitation for her to decide for herself and his withholding of conclusions or personal beliefs heightened her interest in exploring and bringing herself to learning. She continued to explain, however, that connection to peers and the instructor was crucial in this transformation:

> The atmosphere created inside his classroom was one of understanding. Dividing the class into small groups the professor would initiate discussions. The small groups helped break down some of the barriers such as not knowing others in the class and allowed everyone to participate without feeling threatened. I was timid at first and I remember being reluctant to talk about my ideas and interpretations, but I quickly warmed up to group discussions. I found myself openly expressing my opinions. I always felt that my opinions were respected, not only by my classmates but also the professor. The lines of communication were always open between students and the professor. He seemed to enjoy our input and when we had

error in our line of thought he never talked down to us. Through the discussions I gained new ideas and perspectives from other students. I began to have the ability to see issues from all sides of the argument. This not only helped in the classroom setting but in all other aspects of my life. (Baxter Magolda, 2004a, p. 54)

Respect for students' ideas and interpretations made Erin comfortable in expressing her ideas and helped her discover the value of mutually constructing knowledge. She ended her story with these comments:

I am thankful that I enrolled in this class my first semester even though it was not recommended. It didn't kill me but much made me a more responsible student. I walked away at the end of the semester with a new attitude toward learning. I no longer take things as I hear them but I compile information from many sources to evaluate them in order to apply them to my life. Because of the thoughtful information, the open atmosphere, and stylistic changes in the class structure I was able to gain a new perspective on learning. I learned to question authority. (Baxter Magolda, 2004a, pp. 54–55)

Erin's story demonstrates that a carefully crafted learning partnership that blends autonomy and connection has powerful effects on challenging authority dependence.

Challenging authority dependence is particularly difficult in mathematics, a subject in which students have been socialized to believe in certainty and in which pedagogy is often disconnected from students' experience. Sam Rivers, the instructor of the mathematics course that I observed, used learning partnerships to challenge authority dependence and help students connect to their own and others' thinking. He told students that he wanted them to "be actively engaged in the classroom learning environment, proposing solutions, forming hypotheses, asking questions, even arguing. Your own personal construction of mathematical ideas is our goal" (Baxter Magolda, 1999, p. 140). Melissa, a student in the class, explained how Sam encouraged this active engagement: "He'll give us an idea and some time to start thinking about it or talk about it with other students before we actually dig into it. . . . Sometimes he'll give us little hints and we have to go from there on our own" (pp. 160–161). Sam emphasized taking time to think through ideas and collaborating to build on one another's ideas. In one class discussion,

Melissa figured out the key insight before some of her classmates, and she excitedly began to share it. Sam asked her to hold it until the next class session. She described her reaction:

> I was so excited because I knew what he was talking about and I wanted to share, but at the same time I realized that if I would have been in one of the other students' situations, because I have been there before where I did not exactly know what was going on or what he was looking for. It was kind of good I guess that he gave them an opportunity before somebody just blurted out this is what it is or this is how [it works]. (Baxter Magolda, 1999, p. 161)

Sam's emphasis on the mutual construction of knowledge helped students express their ideas, build on one another's ideas, and work as a community until everyone understood the concept. Thus, his approach balanced autonomy and connection. Asked about her reaction to this course, Melissa said,

> With math, up until now for me, in my own personal experience, there has always been one answer and how you arrive at it. [Sam is] trying to [help us] see that there is more than one possible answer or one possible solution. It gives you an opportunity to be creative and to try things. Sure you may be discouraged at times but I think it is very rewarding when you do come up with something and get excited and a lot of times the ideas just start flowing and you don't want to stop or put it down so it's kind of exciting. (Baxter Magolda, 1999, p. 160)

Having knowledge portrayed as complex and socially constructed helped Melissa and her peers begin to form their own construction of mathematics. The connection to their own and others' ideas made mathematics exciting.

Learning Partnerships: Helping Learners Think Interdependently

Helping learners find their own voices and integrate them with those of experts was the focus of the zoology course that I observed. Chris Snowden, the instructor, wanted his students to appreciate the breadth of zoology and its connections to other disciplines. He used examples from his research to show how to approach scientific problems and disparate ideas. His goal was for students "to appreciate what facts really mean. Tentative facts. That's what all of science is. Subject to change and revision" (Baxter Magolda, 1999, p. 103). He wanted them to learn to think like scientists. Erica described how he implemented learning partnerships:

> He takes the approach that he wants you to do it on your own. He will help you plot through your ideas and he will help you sort out what you are thinking and help direct you and he still encourages you to work independently. . . . He'll ask "what are you confused about?" and he will ask your opinion on the matter rather than telling you what you should do. He will ask you exactly what is happening and what you need help with and try to direct you from there rather than presenting himself in a way that is kind of intimidating. . . . he wants you to feel that you are at the same level as him, not in as far as the same knowledge, he wants the atmosphere to be such that you feel comfortable asking him or talking to him in any way. (Baxter Magolda, 1999, pp. 133–134)

Erica's comments illustrate that Chris mutually constructed meaning with students yet encouraged them to take the lead in their learning. Emphasizing the balance between autonomy and connection combined with a supportive teacher-learner relationship helped Erica and her peers think like scientists. They learned to analyze scientific literature and relevant evidence to make judgments.

On a departmental level, the School of Interdisciplinary Studies at Miami University used the LPM to structure a 4-year writing curriculum "to help students progress steadily through three phases, from engagement with expressive modes to an increasingly critical awareness of and proficiency in disciplinary forms to interdisciplinary scholarship" (Haynes, 2004, p. 65). The faculty initially use narratives, personal essays, and autobiographies to entice students to express their own voices. Connection to self as central to knowledge construction is essential to students' progress toward interdisciplinary scholarship, as one faculty member described:

> I am trying to move them away from worrying about what I want to think-ing more about their own ideas. I want them to come up with their own structure, to go to the library and look up other people's ideas, and finally to trust their own judgments and instincts. It is quite a struggle—full of ambiguity, but ultimately the journey can be pretty successful (personal interview, April 9, 2003). (Haynes, 2004, p. 73)

The first-year curriculum validates students' ability to construct ideas, grounds learning in their experience, and portrays learning as a mutual process. The second-year curriculum emphasizes critique, analysis, and integration of disciplinary frameworks, and the third year moves to interdisciplinary scholarship, theory, and practice. As students engage in these increasingly complex tasks, they do so in community. For example, one instructor shared,

> I am always trying to build a community around writing. Students write proposals and reports and post them on the website. Other students must respond to this writing. . . . Moreover, when we have students present their findings, we tell them we will interrupt them at any time to ask questions, to push them to expand upon something. And I tell their classmates to do the same, and ask questions of the presenter. In the beginning, everyone is kind of fearful being up in front of the class and not being able to answer all of the questions posed. So, they are uncomfortable. But as the semester progresses, they become much more comfortable with being uncertain, with having to reason out questions and even saying they don't know the answer and asking their peers for help. Everyone is always asking questions and exchanging ideas (Cummins, personal interview, April 7, 2003). (Haynes, 2004, p. 77)

Junior- and senior-year seminars continue this dual focus on connection and autonomy through collaborative projects and collegial seminar conversations. The senior thesis emphasizes autonomy in crafting the thesis and connection through weekly feedback exchange among peers and faculty regarding the work in progress. The overall curriculum results in students bringing their own voice and experience to the learning process in order to conduct interdisciplinary scholarship for their senior theses.

Learning Partnerships: Integrating Knowledge Construction and Identity

Two contexts revealed the power of sustained efforts to assist learners in coordinating their beliefs, values, and relationships. The Casa de la Solidaridad, a study-abroad program that enables students to live in El Salvador for a semester, integrates academic work with working in the local community. The integration of six academic courses with work in the local community was intentionally organized with the LPM assumptions and principles. The intentional focus on learning partnerships, the intensity of the experience of working in a poor community, and the supportive community established among the Casa staff and students promoted self-authorship. The Casa course assignments required reflection on one's experience, exploration of one's beliefs, and critical analysis of the course topics in the context of the local community. Pam spoke clearly to the role of connection in her own experience at the Casa:

> I had been going to a prestigious university and they have a big focus on thinking analytically and critically and being able to rationalize and reason and have arguments. It is a very certain style of academic thinking. And I had gotten better at that from writing my papers and participating in class and along with that I had always cared about poverty and justice issues. But it was more just from a compassionate emotional intuitive thing, and I think in the Casa, from the things we were reading, the people we were talking to, I started to see those two converge. Like applying the tools of analysis and academic thinking to the issues we were looking at in El Salvador and seeing the immense importance of that . . . So I think, more than anything, just applying these academic tools to what was happening in El Salvador and also at the same time, recognizing the values of different ways of thinking. How you can know things from your experience. You can know things from your faith and spirituality and those ways of thinking should be just as valued, and just as respected as the academic intellectual type of thinking. So ideally, to work on issues like the ones we saw in El Salvador, there should be a convergence of different ways of thinking and they should all be valued. (Yonkers-Talz, 2004, p. 182–183)

Pam's reflection reveals the importance of merging critical analysis, thinking, and reasoning with learners' experience and identity. Although she became skilled in the former modes of thought through her university education, her ability to connect to her own experience and identity stemmed from experiencing the learning partnership of the Casa. This blend of autonomy and connection helped her move beyond the abstract process of academic reasoning to the internalized process of self-authorship.

A master's program offered another example of the influence of an intentional focus on both connection and autonomy. The curriculum and pedagogy of the 2-year, 48-credit student-affairs preparation program intentionally used the LPM to promote self-authorship. As students studied culture and developmental and organizational theory, they were also asked to study their own belief systems, identity, and relations with others. Assignments routinely involved bringing one's experience to knowledge construction, self-reflection, and collaboration with a community of scholars to construct knowledge. One student shared this reaction:

> During my first semester of classes, I was challenged to look at who I was, what I wanted to accomplish, and what I needed to get there. I shared my experiences with my classmates and faculty and felt listened to and an active member of the community. Instead of being given the answers or validation to my fears, I was given the forum to explore the deep down beliefs and principles that guide me. Also, I was able to hear from other members of the community that they felt the same way and we were able to support each other and learn together through these large questions. (Rogers, Magolda, Baxter Magolda, & Knight-Abowitz, 2004, p. 242)

This comment conveys a focus on autonomy—the importance for students to examine and refine themselves, their goals, and the principles that guide them. Simultaneously, it conveys a focus on connection—to one's inner beliefs and to others in a learning community to aid the journey toward self-authorship. This combined emphasis has powerful effects, as noted by this graduate:

> In all, our CSP community has challenged me to evaluate my dreams, my hopes, and myself, to step back from various situations and truly explore the likelihood of creating a certain event or program, to learn to stand for my beliefs, and yet, to also respectfully question others'. My experiences at Miami have challenged me, but they have also helped me to see and to understand who I am to the core. . . . I am grateful to the community we have created, to the space I found for myself, and to the voice I found within me. (Rogers et al., 2004, p. 243)

Ultimately, by combining connection to oneself and connection to others, learning partnerships enable self-authorship. These examples reveal the necessity of promoting both connection and autonomy in higher education.

Designing Learning Partnerships: Implications for Pedagogical Practice and Policy

The extensive narratives from which the LPM emerged reinforce and extend a long history of scholarship on pedagogy, learning, and development.

Synthesizing the evolution of feminist pedagogy, Frances Maher (2002) notes the similarities between feminist pedagogy, Dewey's progressive student-centered approach, and Freire's empowerment of learners. She also emphasized feminists' focus on students' "position"—their learning styles and their cultural and class histories—and the way that positionality mediates knowledge construction. Maher portrays feminist professors as regarding "classroom authority as not fixed but rather as a set of relations that can be acknowledged as grounded in teachers and students evolving various connections to each other and the material" (p. 133). This complex engagement of learners' and educators' histories, identities, and experiences yields pedagogical practice that blends connection and autonomy. Because this engagement welcomes students from their unique and varied positions, it reflects what Gloria Ladson-Billings (1994) calls "culturally relevant pedagogy." The assumptions and principles of the LPM offer a structure through which to craft relations with learners that are inclusive of gender, culture, and class socialization yet invite learners to evolve. These learning partnerships assist students in connecting to their own histories and identities to empower their voices.

The assumptions and principles of the LPM also offer a structure to refine and implement the constructive-developmental pedagogy literature. Belenky et al. (1986) translated Jean Piaget's and William Perry's constructive-developmental approach to connected teaching that aids students in giving birth to their own ideas. Robert Kegan (1994) combined respect for learners' current ways of making meaning with facilitating more complex ways of making meaning. Patricia King and Karen Kitchener (2002), based on their 20-year research program, advanced seven principles for promoting reflective thinking that emphasize respect for students' meaning making, engagement in ill-structured problems, and practicing reflective thinking. The LPM reinforces the tenets of these and other constructive-developmental scholars and brings to the foreground the assumptions about educator and learner authority that are required to engage in inclusive, respectful, learning partnerships.

Crafting learning partnerships requires educators to design educational practice to both welcome and facilitate learners' ways of making meaning. This process begins with analyzing what ways of constructing beliefs, values, and relationships are required of learners in order to achieve particular learning goals. Comparing these demands to learners' current meaning-making capacities unearths developmental goals that are inherent in the learning goals. Once these developmental goals are articulated, it is possible to design a developmental progression that begins with learners' current capacities and moves forward toward the developmental and learning goals much like the writing curriculum noted earlier. The three assumptions and three principles help educators intentionally devise pedagogical relations that respect learners' current meaning making yet invite learners to reconstruct their beliefs, values, and relationships in more complex terms. This approach to pedagogy requires intentionally exploring the developmental demands of one's learning goals and the current capacities of one's students. This teaching method alters the role of educator from providing learners with information and skills to collaborating with them to reconstruct their ways of making meaning. It alters the philosophy that the teacher is the sole authority in favor of mutual negotiation to construct more adequate perspectives. Engaging in learning partnerships extends beyond a few techniques that involve students in activity and discussion; it requires a transformation in educators' thinking about the role of authority, the nature of learning, and the role of learners in the educational process.

The LPM has implications that go beyond educator-learner relationships to the institutional dynamics necessary to support them. Terry Wildman's (2004) story of Virginia Tech's efforts to use the LPM in faculty development and curricular reform makes this point:

> One of the first things we discover in our attempts to introduce new practices in institutional settings is that the *old designs run deep.* Indeed they are embodied in the classrooms where knowledge is *delivered,* in the curriculum practices where requirements are *checked off,* in the space utilization policies where time is *parsed out* in small manageable chunks, in the textbooks where knowledge is carefully *scripted and de-contextualized,* and even in the organizational structures where disciplines can be *isolated* and protected within their own departments. (pp. 250–251, italics in original)

Wildman's description reveals that nearly every aspect of the higher education enterprise is designed in opposition to learning partnerships, in part because higher education has favored autonomy over connection. Yet Wildman also shares the powerful effects of sustained conversations in faculty development settings, learning community initiatives, and curricular reform efforts that help educators surface the frames that restrict their work in order to challenge them. As Wildman observes, the LPM prompts a reexamination of the fundamental workings of the system itself.

Rebecca Mills and Karen Strong (2004) offer an example of just such a reexamination in the context of their reorganization of the Division of Student Life at the University of Nevada, Las Vegas. In their aim to transform "a highly independent, departmentally focused division of student affairs into what is an emerging, interdependent, student-focused learning organization" (p. 269), they engaged their staff in an intensive exploration of their current organization and mutually crafted a new organization that promoted self-authorship for staff and students. Their story demonstrates that using the LPM assumptions and principles welcomed staff members' current ways of making meaning yet facilitated more complex ways of envisioning their work. The staff collectively designed new ways of configuring departments and functions to enhance student learning, articulated new roles for staff, and renegotiated their ways of interacting to achieve their goals. Although Mills and Strong acknowledge the challenges in this learning organization (e.g., time for conversation, reflection, learning, group negotiations), they report numerous examples of its benefit to staff and students.

The fact that old designs run deep—for institutions, educators, and learners—is all the more reason that educators should challenge them. The old designs were crafted for a homogeneous population. Now that research has unearthed the connection inherent in learning for women, students of color, and even for many men, new inclusive designs are essential. Enabling all students, regardless of gender, class, and race, to develop the self-authorship demanded of them in contemporary society is our educational responsibility. Learning partnerships offer one means to meet that responsibility.

References

Association of American Colleges and Universities. (2002). *Greater expectations: A new vision of learning as a nation goes to college*. Washington, DC: Author.

Baxter Magolda, M. B. (1992). *Knowing and reasoning in college: Gender-related patterns in students' intellectual development*. San Francisco: Jossey-Bass.

Baxter Magolda, M. B. (1999). *Creating contexts for learning and self-authorship: Constructive-developmental pedagogy*. Nashville, TN: Vanderbilt University Press.

Baxter Magolda, M. B. (2001). *Making their own way: Narratives for transforming higher education to promote self-development*. Sterling, VA: Stylus.

Baxter Magolda, M. B. (2004a). Learning Partnerships Model: A framework for promoting self-authorship. In M. B. Baxter Magolda & P. M. King (Eds.), *Learning partnerships: Theory and models of practice to educate for self-authorship* (pp. 37–62). Sterling, VA: Stylus.

Baxter Magolda, M. B. (2004b). Self-authorship as the common goal of 21st century education. In M. B. Baxter Magolda & P. M. King (Eds.), *Learning partnerships: Theory and models of practice to educate for self-authorship* (pp. 1–35). Sterling, VA: Stylus.

Baxter Magolda, M. B., & King, P. M. (Eds.). (2004). *Learning partnerships: Theory and models of practice to educate for self-authorship.* Sterling, VA: Stylus.

Belenky, M., Clinchy, B. M., Goldberger, N., & Tarule, J. (1986). *Women's ways of knowing: The development of self, voice, and mind.* New York: Basic Books.

Chickering, A. W. (1969). *Education and identity.* San Francisco: Jossey-Bass.

Gilligan, C. (1982). *In a different voice.* Cambridge, MA: Harvard University Press.

Haynes, C. (2004). Promoting self-authorship through an interdisciplinary writing curriculum. In M. B. Baxter Magolda & P. M. King (Eds.), *Learning partnerships: Theory and models of practice to educate for self-authorship* (pp. 63–90). Sterling, VA: Stylus.

Hillenburg, E. (2002, November). *Response to Transforming Pedagogy to Transform Learning.* Presentation at the Association of American Colleges and Universities Faculty Work and Student Learning Conference, Indianapolis, IN.

Jordan, J. V. (2004). Toward competence and connection. In J. V. Jordan, M. Walker, & L. M. Hartling (Eds.), *The complexity of connection: Writings from the Stone Center's Jean Baker Miller training institute* (pp. 11–27). New York: Guilford Press.

Josselson, R. (1996). *Revising herself: The story of women's identity from college to midlife.* New York: Oxford University Press.

Kegan, R. (1994). *In over our heads: The mental demands of modern life.* Cambridge, MA: Harvard University Press.

King, P. M., & Kitchener, K. S. (2002). The Reflective Judgment Model: Twenty years of research on epistemic cognition. In B. K. Hofer & P. R. Pintrich (Eds.), *Personal epistemology: The psychology of beliefs about knowledge and knowing* (pp. 37–61). Mahwah, NJ: Erlbaum.

Kohlberg, L. (1984). *Essays on moral development: Vol. 1. The philosophy of moral development.* New York: Harper & Row.

Ladson-Billings, G. (1994). *The dreamkeepers: Successful teachers of African American children.* San Francisco: Jossey-Bass.

Maher, F. A. (2002). Feminist pedagogy. In A. M. Martínez Alemán & K. A. Renn (Eds.), *Women in higher education: An encyclopedia* (pp. 130–135). Santa Barbara, CA: ABC-CLIO.

Miller, J. B., Jordan, J. V., Kaplan, A. G., Stiver, I. P., & Surrey, J. L.. (1997). Some misconceptions and reconceptions of a relational approach. In J. V. Jordan (Ed.), *Women's growth in diversity: More writings from the Stone Center* (pp. 25–49). New York: Guilford Press.

Mills, R., & Strong, K. L. (2004). Organizing for learning in a division of student affairs. In M. B. Baxter Magolda & P. M. King (Eds.), *Learning partnerships: Theory and models of practice to educate for self-authorship* (pp. 269–302). Sterling, VA: Stylus.

Perry, W. G. (1970). *Forms of intellectual and ethical development in the college years: A scheme.* Troy, MO: Holt, Rinehart, & Winston.

Rogers, J. L., Magolda, P. M., Baxter Magolda, M. B., & Knight-Abowitz, K. (2004). A community of scholars: Enacting the Learning Partnerships Model in graduate education. In M. B. Baxter Magolda & P. M. King (Eds.), *Learning partnerships: Theory and models of practice to educate for self-authorship* (pp. 213–244). Sterling, VA: Stylus.

Wildman, T. M. (2004). The Learning Partnerships Model: Framing faculty and institutional development. In M. B. Baxter Magolda & P. M. King (Eds.), *Learning partnerships: Theory and models of practice to educate for self-authorship* (pp. 245–268). Sterling, VA: Stylus.

Yonkers-Talz, K. (2004). A learning partnership: U.S. college students and the poor in El Salvador. In M. B. Baxter Magolda & P. M. King (Eds.), *Learning partnerships: Theory and models to educate for self-authorship* (pp. 151–184). Sterling, VA: Stylus.

3

EFFECTIVE PRACTICES IN FOSTERING DEVELOPMENTAL GROWTH IN WOMEN LEARNERS

A View from Neurophysiology

Kathleen Taylor and Catherine Marienau

I think what I have learned overall . . . is how to recognize, understand, use, evaluate and preserve different aspects of my personal power . . . and as a result have more personal peace. . . . "I don't know" has become a more acceptable answer for me.[1]

If I don't know where the heck I've been, I don't know where I am, and I don't know where I can go. And now I feel . . . that there's absolutely no reason why I can't *feel* the way I feel . . . and why I can't choose to do or live or to do things I want. (Lamoreaux, 2005, p. 93)

As I take in new and varying information, internal questions bubble. . . . my internal mental processes are becoming more productive. But having the gear does not mean that I can climb the mountain. That takes practice. I am painfully aware that I am still in training.

Thee are the voices of women embarked on a journey of transformation through learning. They might have come to higher education
merely to acquire a "piece of paper"—a stepping-stone to a better
job, more pay—or perhaps for the personal satisfaction of finishing something left undone. But along the way, something changed. At first, perhaps,
it may have seemed to them that the changes originated with their families,
their workplaces, and their communities. Eventually they came to realize
that it was *they* who had transformed and, in so doing, unsuspectingly
changed those around them.

In 1995, we edited a book called *Learning Environments for Women's
Adult Development: Bridges Toward Change* (Taylor & Marienau). The conceptual framework was drawn from constructive-development theory, primarily Kegan's (1994) "orders of consciousness" model and *Women's Ways of
Knowing* (Belenky, Clinchy, Goldberger, & Tarule, 1997/1986). Essentially,
we and the colleagues who contributed to that volume explored how educators could encourage developmental growth in reentry women learners. How
could we—as faculty, mentors, and women—most effectively support these
students' journey toward greater epistemological complexity?

Our book included explorations of journaling, self-assessment, prior
learning assessment, learning based on personal narrative, and the role of
the mentor. Though each of these was supported by appropriate citations to
existing literature, the research was drawn primarily from other educators'
experiences—largely anecdotal evidence (like our own), which had through
the eloquence or stature of the writers become accepted in our field.

As with most explorations of what goes on inside people's heads, the
study of education has long been relegated to the ranks of "soft" science. But
in the past ten years, the field of neurophysiology has begun to explain in
"hard" scientific terms what it is that the brain does when it remembers,
learns, and changes. It is within this new framework that we now revisit
themes described in the earlier volume. We will attempt to describe why,
based on how the brain functions, certain educational experiences are likely
to change the brain in ways associated with constructive-developmental
growth.[2]

A Mini-Lesson on the Neurophysiology of the Brain

All learning begins with experience. It may not be what we commonly think
of as *having* an experience, because it may register only at a nonconscious

level. Nevertheless, in response to some internal or external event, change occurs at the somatic level in blood pressure, heart rate, hormone production, and so on.

According to Damasio (1999), such changes trigger emotions, which play a role in helping the organism maintain itself by engaging in survival-oriented behaviors. The initiating event and the emotions it engenders—as well as all the related body changes—are stored in the brain. As the brain processes new experiences, it does so analogically—it determines (rightly or wrongly) how the current experience is related to what has gone before. New experiences are therefore connected to existing memories in weblike neuronal patterns that are continuously refined and expanded as we reconstruct memories and the emotional reactions that accompanied them.

The advantage to our species is that not everything must be examined and evaluated de novo—we can use existing patterns based on prior experience to respond to a similar situation. (This was probably very useful the second time a cave-dwelling ancestor faced a saber-toothed tiger.) The disadvantage is that, based on a tenuous similarity, we may respond ineffectively or inappropriately to what is, in fact, a novel situation.

For example, when a reentry adult woman sets foot in a classroom, she brings with her images and emotions connected with earlier school experiences: "we recall not just sensory characteristics . . . but [our] past reactions" to that experience (Damasio, 1999, p. 161). If it was a positive experience, we release hormones and neurotransmitters that lead to a sense of well-being and open ourselves to possibility. If, however, it was a negative experience, we release again the chemical signals that prepare us to fight or flee, whether or not we consciously remember what happened earlier.

When the neuronal patterns stored in the brain effect these body changes, including changes to other parts of the brain, what had been an unconscious emotion passes the threshold into awareness as a *feeling*. At some point in our development—both as a species and for each of us as individuals—the experience of having feelings leads to the wondrous discovery that *someone* is having these feelings. In other words, according to Damasio (1999), the "feeling of what happens" gives rise to the sense of a "self"—when we perceive our emotions and also observe ourselves in the act of perceiving them, we become creatures of *consciousness,* rather than simply creatures of experience (p. 10). Thus, we no longer simply respond to internal or external stimuli but instead develop a sense of ourselves as entities who can control, to some degree, what and how we feel and think.

The Dawn of Consciousness

The notion of how the *self* comes into being was among many things about the workings of the brain that we did not understand when we edited our volume in 1995. We were hardly alone in this lack of understanding. It was long believed that there was a homunculus area somewhere in the brain that "knew" and directed what the brain was doing. The logical impossibility of this (who or what was directing the homunculus?) seemed to escape notice for quite some time. Recent neuroanatomical discoveries confirm that there is no such entity. Instead, there is a complex series of biochemical reactions that call up previously stored images—often at a nonconscious level—and their somatic associations. As Gladwell (2005) has demonstrated, people need not be aware that they have certain knowledge—they may not know why or even that they know something—to be able to call on it.

Eventually, however, the same series of biochemical reactions that enable us to tap into existing neural webs can lead us to awareness that we "have" knowledge and that *we ourselves are the source* of this knowledge. In other words, starting with the brain's need to regulate our life processes continually, and moving through increasingly complex patterns of response including emotions and feelings, we eventually develop the "complex, flexible, and customized plans of response" that are associated with a sense of self and that we call consciousness (Damasio, 1999, p. 55). In essence, as we come to realize consciously what we know, we also develop awareness *that* we know; having recognized ourselves as knowers, we also have the capacity to see that we are constructors of knowledge.

How the Brain Changes

To sustain life successfully, the brain (and nervous system) must learn to cope with an astonishing variety of environmental factors, many of which it has not previously encountered. Because the homeostatic margin of error is relatively small, we must use each learning experience to the fullest. We must therefore do more than simply get better at handling a repetition of *this* particular experience; we must somehow use that experience to anticipate and prepare for future, as yet unseen and unknowable, possibilities. Regardless what your resident teenager may claim, as a species, we cannot afford to learn only by experiencing everything for ourselves. Learning and change are therefore inextricably intertwined.

At the most basic level, learning is a change in the way the brain responds—that is, a change in one's neural networks—based on new information and new stimuli. There are two kinds of such changes. When certain neural networks are repeatedly activated or reactivated, they create stronger connections. As Edelman and Tononi (2000) describe it, "neurons that fire together, wire together" (p. 83). But in addition to strengthening existing patterns, which enables us to store and retrieve images and emotions (the stuff of memory) more effectively, we can also alter existing neural patterns in ways that can make us more flexible and creative in future situations. There is a crucial adaptive balancing act between the two types of changes. On the one hand, we need the well-honed patterns that have so far proven effective in keeping the organism functioning. But we also need to adapt to a rapidly changing environment, in which we are constantly facing situations that challenge the limits of our existing knowledge/memory/experience base and our current beliefs and assumptions.

But, as mentioned earlier, even the storage of "new" data is based on retrieving and using existing patterns. As an example, one of us discovered, after listening to a radio broadcast of *The NewsHour With Jim Lehrer* while driving, that watching the televised broadcast of the same program later that day evoked precise images of the earlier car trip. When Jim Lehrer began the news of the day the second time, and despite the fact that the TV provided competing visual images, it triggered a vibrant flashback of stopping to make a right-hand turn at a particular corner and noticing a child in a pink sweater waiting at the crosswalk—*exactly what had been happening at that point* in the earlier broadcast. (Even now, many months later, writing this description revives those images!) Such immediate and specific access to the somatic responses of an earlier experience may be one source of our success as a species.

To put it another way, those early hominids whose brains were more effective at rapidly calling up and making use of previous experiences were also probably more likely to live long enough to reproduce, thus becoming our ancestors. However, this approach can lead to problems when we do not realize that the "similarities" may be superficial and that *this* experience is actually quite different from *that* experience.

Narrative, Learning, and Self

Nevertheless, the story of our experience is crucially important to our adult development—telling our story can inform our awareness of ourselves as storyteller. We begin to discriminate between the knower and the known and to sense that there is a self doing the knowing. Though it seems to us that the story is verbal, the translation of images and somatic response *into* words, though almost immediate, follows the "nonverbal narrative of consciousness" (Damasio, 1999, p. 185).

In essence, as we tell and retell our stories—whether internally (often unconsciously) or externally (with intention and awareness)—we have the opportunity to reframe them. This "rewiring" of existing associations can substantively change how we approach future experiences. We learn that we are not merely the sum of what has gone before and that new choices and new possibilities are open to us, as one woman discovered:

> But the real gift of this class was having the opportunity to tell my story and see the relevance it has in the real world—the world outside of [my career]. Sometimes I get scared that my life is made up of [that] alone and that without [it] I have no identity. . . . Now I realize that while most of my life does somehow relate to [my career], the experience doesn't stop there. . . . Somehow, I didn't see this before; but now, because of the way this class asked me to evaluate my life experiences, I am able to look at my past and realize the relevance my [other] experiences hold. Because of this, the thought of a career change isn't so scary.

This aspect of narrative or storytelling is effectively used by many counselors, and it also underscores the potential for such teaching and learning strategies as autobiography, journaling/self-assessment, and, as was the case in this particular class, prior learning (portfolio) essays. In each case, thoughtfully describing experiences, memories, and reactions—whether those of this hour, last week, or many years ago—and capturing them in written form creates an opportunity, through reflection and analysis, to change existing patterns of neural networks.

Narrative

Autobiography, as we use it in our courses, is not limited to a formal, lengthy description of the student's life history. Many courses can include a description of earlier experiences that relate to course content. For example, an exploration of one's experiences as a parent, child, or spouse; connections to actual historical events; or familial understandings around money, budgets, credit, and so on can be valuable in courses as varied as psychology, history, and economics. Whatever the topic, when women are encouraged to recapture and review their experience, they often find themselves not only making new meaning of what came before but also thinking differently about the present and future, as the following excerpts suggest:

> I have discovered that I have a whole lot more choice about what happens in my life than I realized. . . . I can now acknowledge that there is a part of me that is not defined by my job, or my function, or my role.

> I would like to begin to acknowledge my strengths and values that are uniquely mine versus what I have been programmed to believe that I am "supposed" to be and do. Writing the autobiography, I can see now that I did not have a good sense of "self." I made decisions based on others' opinions rather than my own. I allowed others' judgments to trigger my self-judgment.

Bringing a woman's personal history to the forefront of awareness helps to make explicit aspects of herself that were formerly implicit and may be associated with helping her form and maintain a sense of self (LeDoux, 2002), which is a hallmark of developmental growth. We have also found that this potential for change and growth is enhanced when we provide a framework for a woman's reflections—specifically, female-based and female-inclusive models of women's development. These may include ways-of-knowing perspectives (Belenky et al., 1997/1986) and relational models (Miller, 1986; Peck, 1986; Surrey, 1991). When we revisit our earlier volume with our current understandings of brain function, we understand more clearly why so many of our women students, such as the one who wrote the following, have found these reflective approaches empowering and growthful:

> When our teacher said that we would be changed people by the end of the semester after [going] through the [autobiographical reflection] process, I, frankly, did not believe it. I thought, "How could I become a changed person from writing more about myself? One thing I know is that I will be a bored person." . . . The word "change" does not do justice to what has happened to me as a result of this class. I did not find a new me. I found the old me who I loved and did not know how much I missed.

Journaling and self-assessment encourage a similar kind of reflection. In both cases, the learner is situated at the center of her own learning process as an observer and interpreter of experience as well as the agent of her future actions. As she enters into a "dialogical relationship" to herself (Taylor, Marienau, & Fiddler, 2000), she can more clearly and consciously articulate her beliefs and values as well as thoughtfully evaluate the ideas and actions that arise from them. For example:

> [Journaling] helps me map out my thoughts and how I felt about a certain situation at that point in time. Later, I am able to look back and understand why I felt that way . . . and what I have done or not done to improve the situation. I then evaluate the situation again to see how important it is and whether or not I should do something to improve it.

Both activities also powerfully support learning from experience (Boud, Keogh & Walker, 1985)—which is another way of saying creating changes in neural patterns. As a result, learners can take new perspectives on previous experiences, change their current behaviors, and commit to new courses of future actions (Marienau, 1999).

> I used self-assessment to reflect . . . about a particularly challenging experience. I looked for my part in it. I did not take the attitude of blaming others or having self pity. I felt I was making a pretty clean observation. . . . what self-assessment means to me is taking an objective look at your performance, attitudes and effort. I find that the value of self-assessment is that it forces me to look at the truth about my efforts. The value of that is that I can see where I need to possibly learn more and work harder.

In a recent study that one of us conducted on the effects of self-assessment (Marienau, 1999), participants described a shift from an external to an internal frame of reference, increased self-acceptance and self-esteem, a heightened sense of competence, and increased abilities to communicate, work with others, make decisions, and pursue realistic goals, as well as feeling more in charge of their personal and professional lives and of having clearer life direction (p. 144). All of these effects suggest that existing patterns of self-understanding were altered in favor of patterns that support greater self-agency and self-authorship—in other words, developmental growth.

The structured learning journal, as described by both Walden (1995) and Marienau (1995), is an even more focused approach. With structured learning journals, instructors frame questions that prompt students to reflect on their own experience in light of the readings and group discussions, with the intention that they interpret their experience—and those of others—in a broader context. For example, the following excerpt, from a journal assignment that asked management students to brainstorm and then reflect on times when they had been ineffective in the workplace, strongly suggests that the assignment has challenged existing patterns of belief and behavior:

> It was difficult for me "the perfectionist" to think about what I do to make ME less effective at work. Well, at the beginning of my brainstorm I did not want to see it, but what an eye opener to look at myself in the work setting. I never thought there was anything that I needed to change until now. . . . I seem to wait for mistakes to happen, that way I can immediately jump on [people] two seconds after they occur. I set out to look for the things that will go wrong.

The importance of narrative also surfaced in Lamoreaux's (2005) research on prior learning assessment (PLA). When we wrote, in 1995, that the PLA process encourages development, we were extrapolating from what we saw our learners experience and from the developmental literature (Droegkamp & Taylor, 1995). In Lamoreaux's classes, as in many PLA portfolio classes, students petition for credit by writing essays that describe learning that they acquired from extramural personal and professional experiences, using relevant disciplinary lenses as their guide to what counts as "college-level learning." Those first drafts are then revised after the student receives feedback from other students and the instructor. The revised essays are submitted to evaluators whose academic credentials are appropriate to the subject matter.

Now we understand that when the brain "re-creates" an earlier experience, as it does in writing these essays, it does not simply replicate the earlier memory. "In higher organisms, every act of perception is, to some degree, an act of creation, and every act of memory is, to some degree, an act of imagination" (Edelman & Tononi, 2000, p. 101). This dynamic is clearly key to the success of the counseling context; it is also why prior learning assessment can encourage the perspective shifts associated with greater complexity of mind.

Lamoreaux's (2005) grounded research study described ways in which "writing about experience, guided by the reflective component" was central to adult learners' experience of change, as it "foster[ed] taking a more objective stance toward one's experience" (p. 123). Three components of narrative writing most affected learners' experience of change: identifying multiple perspectives, writing to know, and seeing experience as object.

In the context of experiential learning theory, writing narratives about their experiences "helped participants to *clarify* and *organize* their knowledge" (Lamoreaux, 2005, p. 129). From a transformative learning perspective, "the process of writing their experience down seemed to foster for many a shift in perspective, looking at their lives from the 'outside in,' instead of 'inside out,' . . . and seeing patterns of which they had been unaware" (Lamoreaux and Taylor, 2006, p. 55). As one woman noted,

> If you're telling a narrative to someone . . . [you can't] go back and look over it again and start to see, *why* did that same thing keep happening? . . . When you look at it on paper . . . you can see patterns. . . . [R]eading these papers over and over . . . gives you that perspective *as if you were somebody else looking at your own life.* (Lamoreaux, 2005, p. 108, emphasis in original)

From a constructivist framework, "narrative is a primary structure through which human beings organize and make meaning of their experience. . . . Meaning is constructed, understood, and expressed in story form" (Rossiter, 1999, p. 61). Lamoreaux (2005) found that learners' writing essays based on personal experience added to their self-knowledge, as illustrated by these quotations from two women learners:

> Writing the papers (especially the one about my mother's passing) was a very cathartic experience. I was able to not only feel my emotions, which ranged from guilt to pain . . . but seeing the words helped me come to grips with the fact that I did the best I could at the time. (p. 77)

> I didn't realize that the way I parented was different from the way that other parents parented. . . . So I think that was a learning *experience* to see that my way was so different than the way I was raised, and that I had made choices to do it differently even though maybe those were subconscious choices. But as I began to go through the course, *I consciously realized why I'd been doing it.* (p. 83, emphasis in original)

Writing personal narratives also prompted learners to see other perspectives:

> Even in the parenting [essay], you had to compare and contrast, so it forced
> you to look at the way *you* parent as *one* way, not just *the* way. . . . I think
> that we just assume that that's the way you do things and when you start
> to look at other ways, I think that opens your . . . world view. You get
> more open-minded. . . . it does open you up to being more accepting of
> other viewpoints. (p. 83, emphasis in original)

And, in some instances, personal narrative affirms a learner's existing convictions, but from a wider view—the student just quoted continues, "I think
because of my religious background, it doesn't change my convictions, but I
think it helps me to understand other people" (p. 83). Such narratives, say
Cozolino and Sprokay (2006), "support memory function and serve as a
guide for future behavior" (p. 13).

Reflection

Narrative, on its own, could conceivably remain one's unchanging story.
What appears to give it power to change the brain is *reflection*—in effect,
holding up a mirror to one's story. Dewey (1944) underscored this when he
said that reflection accepts "responsibility for the future consequences that
flow from present action" (p. 145). It is hardly surprising, then, that the development of reflective skills is key to learning from experience and an essential factor in development. According to Cozolino (2002),

> Reflexive language keeps us in the moment, reacting to stressors in the
> midst of survival. Reflective language demonstrates our ability to escape
> from the present moment, gain perspective on our reflexive actions, and
> make decisions about what and how we would like to change. (pp.
> 293–294)

Cozolino suggests that *reflexive* means reactive, automatic, immediate, and
not thought through; by contrast, *reflective* is considered, deliberate, and
thoughtful. Reflection also takes into account both cognitive and affective
dimensions (Boud, Keogh, & Walker, 1985), as well as the relationship we
have with ourselves and with others in the world.

Mezirow (1991) identifies three forms of reflection. The first is associated
with problem solving and is the basis for the natural sciences: *"How strong*

should the levees be to prevent Katrina-like destruction in the future?" The second looks beyond the content of a particular problem to the context, thus shifting to a wider analysis that invites a more complex analysis: *"What other factors might determine where and whether to build or rebuild?"* The third form, critical reflection, involves taking perspective on the assumptions behind the earlier questions: *"How do our beliefs about and relationship with the natural environment affect our approach to situating and protecting population centers?"* Critical reflection is most likely to lead to developmental growth, as it involves the following:

- Identifying the assumptions that underlie our thoughts and actions
- Scrutinizing how accurate and valid our assumptions are
- Changing our assumptions to make them more inclusive of other perspectives and less narrow or limiting (Tennant & Pogson, 1995, pp. 162–163)

The following quotation from a learner illustrates this interplay among critical thinking, learning, and development:

> Then I tried reflecting on my learning as it was happening, and I became aware for the first time of some of my blind spots—you know, where I wasn't being at all objective about myself or open to someone else's ideas. . . . Because of learning about reflection, and learning to do it, I am now willing to listen to another person's perspective and weigh it; I'm asking others for feedback about myself, especially at work, and I can do more generalizing—I'm not so concrete about everything. I just never thought I would have this kind of flexibility. (Taylor et al., 2000, p. 28)

This self-description underscores the fact that critically reflecting on and questioning one's assumptions can lead to changes in how people understand themselves and the world around them. The quotation also accords with Habermas's observation that self-reflection is a "paradoxical achievement [in that] one part of the self must be split off from the other part in such a manner that the subject can be in a position to render aid to itself" (cited in Boud et al., 1985, p. 36)—a philosophical description of the experience described in our earlier volume as the position from which it is possible to "observe myself observing, perceive myself perceiving, and examine myself creating the reality that creates who I am" (Taylor, 1995, p. 22). Cozolino's (2002) more recent description uses the language of neuroscience: "Self-reflection requires both higher levels of affect regulation and cognitive processing" and may promote the "higher levels of neural network integration" (p. 294) that lead to new awareness. In so doing, it may also lead to movement along the continuum associated with greater epistemological complexity.

Mentoring

Mentoring has gained prominence in the adult higher education movement over the past 35 years. Noddings (1984) carefully defined it this way: "Mentors do not only care *about* their students; they also care *for* them by making an effort to understand their experience. Apprehending the other's reality, feeling what he [or she] feels as nearly as possible, is the essential part of caring" (p. 16).

Daloz (1986), who coined the term "teaching as care," emphasized the context of "development of the whole person" (p. xvii), which in his view is the ultimate purpose of the mentoring relationship. Kegan (1994) further underscored this: "the most essential role of the mentor is to provide the holding environment on which all development depends" (p. 287).

Even so, mentoring is not just all about relationship—it involves subject matter and the learner's processing of more complex ways of knowing while trying on the new lenses that will enable seeing and understanding aspects of the world in deeper ways. However, even when the learner-mentor relationship is oriented primarily around subject matter—as in an independent study on genetics or policy analysis—an essential role of the mentor is to provide a holding environment that supports and challenges the learner (in the right balance for that particular person) while sticking around as long as needed (Kegan, 1982, 1994).

In our earlier volume, Mayra Bloom (1995) characterized mentors' roles in terms of how they stand metaphorically in relation to their learners at different points in the educational process: ahead (guiding, leading forward), behind (observing, coaching), face-to-face (questioning, dialoguing), and shoulder-to-shoulder (sharing the journey of learning and growth). This characterization is echoed in Johnson's description, based in cognitive neuro-science and social cognitive neuroscience, of the "intersubjective space" most supportive of learning and growth: "The brain actually needs to seek out an affectively attuned other if it is to learn" (2006, p. 66).

Lamoreaux (2005) provides specific examples of how learners experi-enced a particular kind of faculty feedback as both encouragement and chal-lenge. As one woman explained,

> When [the instructor] would write comments, sometimes I would just think, "but I thought I *answered* that." . . . Her comments would make me go much more deeply into whatever [and realize] that I'd just scratched the surface of something. . . . [W]hat specifically [the instructor] said, I think, was . . . "Who cares, so what, why?" The first time I read the com-ments, it was like, "Geez! . . . I just poured blood, sweat, and tears into this, and she's saying, 'Why, so what, who cares?'" And then you go, "No, no, no, no, this is just *support*." It's like, "well, why *is* this important, and *who does* care about this, and what's the greater truth?" (pp. 112–113)

Given that the "brain is a social organ innately designed to learn through shared experiences" (Cozolino & Sprokay, 2006, p. 11), such supportive yet challenging dialogue fosters learning and development. We are not necessar-ily talking about cognitive interplay between learner and mentor only around interesting and provocative subject matter, though that is valuable and im-portant. The kind of authentic dialogue that promotes development also en-gages the affective dimensions, as one woman reveals in her description of her "unstuffy" professor:

> [He] was the type of teacher that I prefer because he is a human being. You know, he was a human being first. Then he was a teacher, and a lot of people who are that well educated are, well, "I'm a doctor, but I'm a teacher. Then, I'm a person." No. You're a human being first. . . . So, yes, in that regard, getting good feedback was helpful to me because I related to him. (Lamoreaux, 2005, p. 113)

As Zull (2002) explains, the "entire brain is an organ of emotion and . . . emotion, reason, and memory are all linked together" (p. 65). Thus, cognition (our mental process for forming knowledge) is stimulated by the feeling component of an experience: If we do not react and feel, we do not think. There is therefore an interdependent relationship between feeling and thinking, between emotion and cognition—hence Herman and Mandell's (2004) observation that the mentoring relationship is based on a kind of intimacy that they call "cognitive love" (p. 117).

Johnson (2006) confronts head-on the influence of emotions on learning, paying particular attention to emotions such as fear and anxiety—the "negative" ones we adult educators tend to shy away from. While educators are long on encouraging adult learners to engage in more complex ways of knowing, they tend to be short on extending emotional support for the discomfort that adult learners may feel during that process (perhaps because they do not wish to stray into what may appear to be a therapeutic mode—see Johnson & Taylor, 2006, for a fuller description of the similarities and differences between the professional roles of counselor and educator).

However, even learners with adequate skills often experience transformative learning environments as threatening, and less-skilled learners are likely to be even more overwhelmed. Without being consciously aware of doing so, their bodies tense, concentration suffers, and anxiety, impatience, and confusion all increase. The right balance of support and challenge can counteract this tendency toward constriction, thus leading the brain to produce dopamine instead of anxiety-producing chemicals. Rather than a fear-based response, the mentor's efforts can create a situation in which a learner feels good, in control, and able to learn.

Conclusion

The experience of learning, change, and growth was poignantly captured by a woman whom Lamoreaux (2005) identifies as "Mary," who is 53, a professional dancer and dance educator and a cancer survivor. In a journal written early in her program, Mary observed,

> I now realize one of the purposes of this class . . . to get past the stories and traumatic events that keep running one's life, that takes place when one is able to dig as deeply as possible into those uncomfortable and embarrassing places. By slogging through those places, there is a space that can open up for new learning. A new paradigm is possible. I think it's like repotting a plant into a large pot. If the plant stays in the same old pot it can't grow and expand, but it doesn't know that because it's stuck in the

same old crampy pot. In this course we have a chance to move into a bigger pot if we choose. (p. 100)

A year later, during an interview about her ongoing learning experiences, she reflected further:

I definitely feel more mature, feel like I've grown; it's sort of a process of growing up, learning these things about yourself that you've been doing. I think sometimes when we go on our merry way through our lives, through my life—I'm always doing stuff, and doing stuff, and doing stuff—I just stop and look at everything, and open up all these different cans of life. Changes the way I look at it. *I think any time you look at something in great detail, you can't look at [it] the same way.* So that just keeps changing. I can't put all those things back in the can. So I feel more, in the world, I feel more connected to other people, I feel able to do a better job of what I'm doing from really stopping and taking a look at everything. (p. 100, emphasis in original)

Mary's self-description parallels what we now know about how learning can change the brain. Using learning strategies such as narrative, journaling, and self-reflection, while being supported by caring and attuned mentors, Mary has been able to establish new neural networks—or as she puts it, "open up all these different cans of life." As a result, she is no longer in the "same old crampy pot" but has availed herself of the opportunity to choose a different, bigger, pot—one that makes her more effective in many aspects of her personal and professional life.

Learning can change the brains—and therefore the lives—of adults. Teaching and learning strategies that take advantage of our emerging under-standings of how the brain stores, retrieves, and reframes earlier synaptic as-sociations can help to overcome some of the traumatic experiences that have kept adult learners—men and women—from successfully pursuing higher education. We do not mean to suggest that all the challenges we face as adult educators will disappear if only we familiarize ourselves with the basics of brain function, but we have found that it offers support for what many of us have intuitively recognized as "best practices." With that in mind, and with gratitude for the many ways that our learners have enriched our lives, person-ally and professionally, we give Mary the last word: "But I think once the process starts, I don't think it stops. At least for me it hasn't stopped. It just keeps unfolding. Soon I'll be ready to be repotted again" (Lamoreaux, 2005, pp. 100–101).

Notes

1. Uncited quotations are from assignments written for various classes at DePaul University's School for New Learning and Saint Mary's College of California's School of Extended Education.

2. We wish to acknowledge our debt of gratitude to Dr. Sandra Johnson, on whose dissertation committee we both served and who initially pointed us toward these connections.

References

Belenky, M. F., Clinchy, B. M., Goldberger, N. R., & Tarule, J. M. (1997). *Women's ways of knowing: The development of self, voice, and mind* (10th anniversary ed.) New York: Basic Books. (Originally published 1986)

Bloom, M. (1995). Multiple roles of the mentor supporting women's adult development. In K. Taylor & C. Marienau (Eds.), *Learning environments for women's adult development: Bridges toward change* (pp. 63–72). New Directions for Adult and Continuing Education, no. 65. San Francisco: Jossey-Bass.

Boud, D., Keogh, R., & Walker, D. (1985). *Reflection: Turning experience into learning.* New York: Kogan Page.

Cozolino, L. (2002). *The neuroscience of psychotherapy: Building and rebuilding the human brain.* New York: Norton.

Cozolino, L., & Sprokay, S. (2006). Neuroscience and adult learning. In S. Johnson & K. Taylor (Eds.), *The neuroscience of adult learning* (pp. 11–19). New Directions for Adult and Continuing Education, no. 110. San Francisco: Jossey-Bass.

Daloz, L. A. (1999). *Mentor: Guiding the journey of adult learners.* San Francisco: Jossey-Bass.

Damasio, A. (1999). *The feeling of what happens: Body and emotion in the making of consciousness.* Orlando, FL: Harcourt Brace.

Dewey, J. (1944) *Democracy and education.* New York: The Free Press.

Droegkamp, J., & Taylor, K. (1995, Spring). Prior learning assessment, critical self-reflection, and reentry women's development. In K. Taylor & C. Marienau (Eds.), *Learning environments for women's adult development: Bridges toward change* (pp. 29–36). New Directions for Adult and Continuing Education, no. 65. San Francisco: Jossey-Bass.

Edelman, G. M., & Tononi, G. (2000). *A universe of consciousness.* New York: Basic Books.

Gladwell, M. (2005). *Blink: The power of thinking without thinking.* New York: Little, Brown.

Herman, L., & Mandell, A. (2004). *From teaching to mentoring.* New York: RoutledgeFalmer.

Johnson, S. (2006). The neuroscience of the mentor-learner relationship. In S. Johnson & K. Taylor (Eds.), *The neuroscience of adult learning* (pp. 63–71). New Directions for Adult and Continuing Education, no. 110. San Francisco: Jossey-Bass.

Johnson, S., & Taylor, K. (2006). *The neuroscience of adult learning.* New Directions for Adult and Continuing Education, no. 110. San Francisco: Jossey-Bass.

Kegan, R. (1982). *The evolving self: Problems and process in human development.* Cambridge, MA: Harvard.

Kegan, R. (1994). *In over our heads: The mental demands of modern life.* Cambridge, MA: Harvard University Press.

Lamoreaux, A. (2005). *Adult learners' experience of change related to prior learning assessment.* Unpublished doctoral dissertation, Walden University.

Lamoreaux, A., & Taylor, K. (2006). Prior learning assessment and transformative learning. *All About Mentoring, 31,* 54–57.

LeDoux, J. (2002). *The synaptic self: How our brains become who we are.* New York: Penguin Books.

Marienau, C. (1995). In their own voices: Women learning about their own development. In K. Taylor & C. Marienau (Eds.), *Learning environments for women's adult development: Bridges toward change* (pp. 37–44). New Directions for Adult and Continuing Education, no. 65. San Francisco: Jossey-Bass.

Marienau, C. (1999). Self-assessment at work: Outcomes of adult learners' reflections on practice. *Adult Education Quarterly, 49*(8), 135–146.

Mezirow, J. (1991). *Transformative dimensions of adult learning.* San Francisco: Jossey-Bass.

Miller, J. B. (1986). *Toward a new psychology of women* (2nd ed.). Boston: Beacon Press.

Noddings, N.. (1984) *Caring, a feminine approach to ethics & moral education.* Berkeley: University of California Press

Peck, T. (1986). Women's self-definition in adulthood: From a different model? *Psychology of Women Quarterly, 10,* 274–284.

Rossiter, M. (1999). A narrative approach to development: Implications for adult education. *Adult Education Quarterly, 50*(1), 56–71.

Surrey, J. (1991). The self in relation: A theory of women's development. In J. Jordan, A. Kaplan, J. B. Miller, I. Stiver, & J. Surrey, *Women's growth in connection.* New York: Guilford Press.

Taylor, K. (1995, Spring). Sitting beside herself: Self-assessment and women's adult development. In K. Taylor & C. Marienau (Eds.), *Learning environments for women's adult development: Bridges toward change* (pp. 21–28). New Directions for Adult and Continuing Education, no. 65. San Francisco: Jossey-Bass.

Taylor, K., & Marienau, C. (Eds.). (1995) *Learning environments for women's adult development: Bridges toward change.* New Directions for Adult and Continuing Education, no. 65. San Francisco: Jossey-Bass.

Taylor, K., Marienau, C., & Fiddler, M. (2000). *Developing adult learners: Strategies for teachers and trainers.* San Francisco: Jossey-Bass.

Tennant, M. & Pogson, P. (1995). *Learning and change in the adult years.* San Francisco: Jossey-Bass.

Walden, P. (1995, Spring). Journal writing: A tool for women developing as knowers. In K. Taylor & C. Marienau (Eds.), *Learning environments for women's adult development: Bridges toward change* (pp. 13–20). New Directions for Adult and Continuing Education, no. 65. San Francisco: Jossey-Bass.

Zull, J. E. (2002). *The art of changing the brain.* Sterling, VA: Stylus.

4

WOMEN IN
TECHNOLOGY CAREERS

Teri Sosa

W alk into a faculty meeting of the computer science department of any university. Chances are that the majority of the faculty members will be male. Likewise, a look around the software programming department of most companies is likely to reveal many more male than female software engineers. Although women have made gains in technology careers, both in business and academia, they continue to be vastly underrepresented.

Not only are women underrepresented in technology careers, but they are also underrepresented in the educational pathways that lead to those careers. At every step in the journey from education to career, the number of women decreases. The metaphor of a pipeline is frequently used to describe the journey of girls through elementary, junior high, high school, undergraduate, and graduate education to careers in technical fields. Most people who have used this metaphor have described this pipeline as "shrinking" or "leaky" to paint a more vivid picture of attrition as girls and women move from one stage of their education to the next (Alper, 1993; Camp, 1997).

Although girls in elementary school and junior high school usually take a prescribed schedule of classes, the activities they choose outside of school, in spite of their involvement with ubiquitous technology tools such as cell phones, generally do not involve computing (American Association of University Women [AAUW], 2000). As the same girls move into young womanhood and have some choice over their academic programs in the later high school years, they opt out of technology courses in school as well. And significant numbers of young women continue to choose nontechnical fields for their major course of study as they move into higher education. Although the percentage of women enrolled in institutions of higher education has steadily increased since the beginning of the 20th century and continues to rise as we begin the 21st century, the percentage of young women pursuing undergraduate and graduate degrees in the most technical fields remains low compared to the percentage of their male counterparts who do.

This chapter investigates how women arrive at technical careers and attempts to answer the question of why so few women complete the journey. Generally, research of women's pathways to technological careers is conducted from one of two perspectives. One perspective considers the affective or psychological factors that influence women as they determine their educational, social, career, and life goals. For example, researchers who use this perspective to investigate the connection of girls and computer technology may give consideration to the identity issues that young girls face in adolescence, such as peer pressure, self-esteem, and self-image. Adolescent girls may not engage with formal training in technology because it is not what their friends do, it is not cool, or they think it is too hard. Studies that focus on the psychological or affective factors that influence young women as they mature may investigate the self-doubt that young women in high school and college-age women feel when they enroll in computer science programs.

The other perspective for exploration of women's connection with scientific and technological fields takes a more structural view. This perspective examines the interplay of society, culture, and institutions that causes women to be systemically disconnected from technological courses of study and the careers to which they lead. In this context, the institution's focus on programs that disenfranchise women from and devalue women's contribution to technical programs is problematized.

These affective and structural positions differ in their starting point. Whereas the psychological perspective takes the women's personal development and attitudes as a central starting point for investigation, the structural approach centers on external factors. Therefore, the structural position recognizes societal and institutional change as solutions.

Of course, a complete picture of women's connection with technology must examine evidence from both perspectives. The way a woman feels about technology will certainly influence her engagement with high school and college technical studies as well as her choice of careers. Conversely, the degree to which institutions prepare and welcome women influences women's comfort in the field. This chapter is primarily concerned with the programs, policies, and cultural norms that have led to either the inclusion or exclusion of women from technical career paths and therefore takes the institution as the starting point. The focus is on the external structures that encourage or discourage women. Although affective factors that influence women's participation in technological fields are extremely important in the complete study of women's lack of representation, they are considered here only insofar as they have been given as reasons for cultural critique or institutional change.

In considering the societal, cultural, and institutional factors that contribute to the underrepresentation of women in technical occupations, this chapter presents four sections. First, the chapter begins with a discussion and definition of pathways to technical careers. The second section provides a historical analysis of women's institutional interaction with technology education and careers. The third section presents a discussion of the women's pathways to technical occupations in the past 20 years. In the final section of the chapter, some thoughts are put forward about the future of women in technology occupations both in the academy and in industry.

Definition of a Technical Career Path

There is no question that the connection of girls and women to technology is being investigated more now than in the past. What leads girls to (or discourages girls from) careers in information technology? If there is a direct educational pathway, many women who end up in information technology jobs do not even find it. For example, Turner, Bernt, and Pedora's (2002) large study of adult women in information technology fields found that 31% of the women they surveyed had undergraduate degrees in arts, social sciences, or humanities. Another 12% had undergraduate degrees in fields related to computer science, mathematics, and engineering. Further, this significant number of women in information technology jobs (43%) did not pursue formal postbaccalaureate computer science education but instead learned the requirements of their field "on the job." Therefore, it is clear that direct educational pathways are not the only way to enter a computer-related career.

Even though we cannot assert that all pathways to technical careers are academic, we can make some judgments about the existing academic pathways. First, for purposes of this chapter, it is assumed that women who do pursue undergraduate and graduate degrees in computer science intend ultimately to have jobs in information technology fields. Second, it is assumed that undergraduate majors in related fields, such as mathematics and engineering, are more likely to feed into business or academic technology careers than are majors in other areas. Third, it is also clear that academic professions require formal credentialing at the doctoral level and therefore have advanced computer science degrees as their prerequisite.

So, for the purpose of this discussion, the definition of a technical career is employment in a computer-related field. Prerequisite study for such fields, however, may be advanced knowledge of mathematics, engineering, or computer science. With this in mind, this chapter discusses computer science specifically but also adds study of mathematics and engineering where appropriate. In addition, the terms *information technology, technology, computer-based technology,* and *computing* are used interchangeably.

Because the number of studies is increasing, various permutations of math, science, engineering, technology, and social science may be aggregated and reported in ways that present different pictures. For example, when the Higher Education Research Institute surveyed American freshman in 2004 (National Science Foundation, 2006), it found that 26.3% of incoming female freshmen intended to major in "science and engineering" fields. This figure, however, included social and behavioral sciences as a category of science and engineering and also included biology, agricultural, and physical sciences. When the data are disaggregated, only 3.9% of female freshmen (as opposed to 23% of freshman males) intended to major in computer sciences, engineering, or mathematics. And only 0.4% of these undergraduate women specified computer science as their intended undergraduate major. Therefore, we must carefully attend to the data to arrive at a complete picture.

Careful interrogation of newly abundant data suggests that women are still underrepresented at every stage of the pipeline. And whether women reach the end of the pipeline through a direct pathway or an indirect pathway is less important than recognizing and correcting the fact that women are institutionally discouraged from participating in information technology fields at every crossroad.

Historical Background

The definition of technology has not been static. It changed significantly as mechanical inventions increased and has changed even more dramatically with the proliferation of digital inventions. In looking at the educational paths to technical careers, it is important to remember that the history of free public education in America is not the same for women as it is for men, especially White men. Therefore, early institutionalized exclusion of women from educational pathways leading to technology training is not surprising. It is also not surprising to note that even when women were finally able to receive formal training in technology and technology-related fields, they were considered unsuitable employees and systemically discouraged from taking technology-related jobs.

The Evolving Definition of Technology

In considering the institutionalized disconnect of women and technology, it is helpful to understand how technology and technology-related careers attained their current male-dominated status. Because early definitions of technology were much more related to useful inventions of all types, it is instructive to see how the boundaries of technology were narrowed to exclude all but mechanical inventions. In fact, the definition of technology is now commonly limited to the creation, maintenance, and use of digital machines. This section investigates the evolution of the current limited definition of technology and looks at how this narrowed discipline came to be equated with men and machines to the exclusion of women.

Oldenziel (1999) argues that "men's love affair with technology is something we take for granted" (p. 9). This statement begs the question, What are the origins of the male love affair with technology? Were there bounded bodies of knowledge that men came to love, or did men draw boundaries around those things that they loved and call them technology? In other words, do men love technology because they are responsible for its definition?

The answers to these questions have serious implications. Oldenziel (1999), Stanley (1992, 1993), and others (see Koerber, 2000; Spender, 1995) suggest that it is no accident that the definition of technology is drawn in male terms. These authors suggest that men systematically formed the definition of technology in ways that were most comfortable and familiar to them. Often these methods excluded women and things that were important to women.

Historically, the terms "useful arts" and "technology" were used interchangeably (Oldenziel, 1999, p. 14). This broader definition suggests that originally technology was seen as useful knowledge, both physical products and intellectual activity that enhanced everyday life. Machinery was only part of the definition of technology.

In the late 19th and early 20th centuries, however, perhaps in correlation with the Industrial Revolution and the rise of scientific modernism, the definition of technology became equated with applied science, tools, machines, and engineering. First, a transition occurred from technology as useful art to technology as applied science (Oldenziel, 1999). Initially all invention was valued, so inventions such as the corset were still connected with technology. As the new century dawned, however, the nonmechanical and nonpatented came to be excluded from definitions of technology. Technology increasingly became the province of engineers, designers of machines. And these engineers were, and continue to be, predominantly male (U.S. Department of Labor, Women's Bureau, 2002).

Technology bound to engineering evolved as a systematic discipline, centered on common, mathematically oriented principles. The more creative aspects of engineering and technology were subordinated to the mechanical aspects (Ambrose, Dunkle, Lazarus, Nair, & Harkus, 1997).

As this shift occurred and technology came to be understood as more mathematical, more systematic, more linear, more abstract, and less creative, women became increasingly estranged from it. First, the definition of technology narrowed, with inventions and technologies most useful to women being removed. Second, those responsible for producing the remaining technology did not allow women to have a part in its production. Women who ventured into the newly redefined technologies were not seen as acceptable producers of technology.

> Because it draws on science, technology has traditionally been considered as falling within the realm of "men's work." The traditional view of the inherent masculinity of science and technology combined with the entrenched idea that a woman's place is in the home, often prevented women from participating in technological endeavors and from receiving due recognition when they did venture to participate. The contributions of

women to technology were often overlooked. (Zierdt-Warshaw, Winkler, & Bernstein, 2000, p. xi)

In addition to societal barriers, institutional barriers also made it difficult for women to participate in technical fields. For example, in engineering fields, in the late 19th century and well into the 20th century, professional organizations and licensing systems made it more difficult for women to obtain the proper credentials (Oldenziel, 1999). Those women who did succeed in technical fields often did so by aligning with a husband or father who was successful. In this way, a woman was able to participate almost as a surrogate, invisible for her own contributions, riding on a man's coattails.

Women were able to work as engineers if they learned the trade through their families or husbands. For example, Emily Warren Roebling completed projects under her husband's name during the 1870s and 1880s. When her husband, a chief engineer on the Brooklyn Bridge, became ill, she acted as a proxy and worked toward the bridge's completion. Thus, it was only through her husband's connection, not through recognition of her talents, that Emily Roebling was able to be a practicing engineer (Oldenziel, 1999).

As the definition of technology became more oriented toward tools, devices, and systems and more specialized to professions such as engineering and computer science, the link between technology and masculinity got stronger (see Koerber, 2000). And as computers became more prevalent, the definition of technology further extended to cover all aspects of computer culture (Woodfield, 2000).

Because it was not acceptable for women to produce technology for much of the early 20th century, women's achievements were underreported, even when they fit into the categories of acceptable technology (Stanley, 1993).

The Computer Age

When we discuss computer technology, it is important to remember that digital technology is a relatively new field. Although mechanical computers and computer programming trace their origins to Charles Babbage and Ada Lovelace in the early 19th century (Otterbein University, n.d.), the history of modern computing generally begins with the first use of the ENIAC (Electronic Numerical Integrator and Calculator) in 1946 (Otterbein University).

Ironically, the ENIAC's first computer programmers were women who programmed the computer from wiring diagrams (Otterbein University, n.d.). As business uses for the computer became more evident, however, demand for computer programmers increased. The ranks of programmers were quickly populated by men and transformed into a high-status profession.

By the late 1960s the number of programmers had grown to approximately 300,000 (Jensen, 1967). It was clear that there were not enough trained programmers to fill all the open positions. People would need to be trained in programming, and a tool for identifying programming potential in prospective programmers was necessary. The programming aptitude test was that tool.

Most of the early programming aptitude tests were developed by manufacturers of computer hardware. In the 1960s the two largest commercial manufacturers of computers were IBM and Univac. Each manufacturer developed its own programmer aptitude test. In 1967, the two most widely used tests were the IBM Aptitude Test for Programmer Personnel and the Univac Programmer Aptitude Battery, with the IBM test used about 75% to 80% of the time (Jensen, 1967).

Analysis of these gate-keeping tests shows that the tests favor analytical, linear thinkers. Some observers have questioned whether a high score on these tests was actually a predictor of future success in programming (Costa, 1998). If it is true that those who have a learning style that allows them to score well on the programming aptitude test will be good programmers, is it equally true that those who have learning styles that are not compatible with scoring well will be poor programmers? This is a difficult question. Testing this hypothesis would require hiring people who did not score well on tests and assessing their performance. It seems unlikely that this type of testing would occur in a corporate or academic environment.

Although data relating to learning style, programming aptitude, and programming achievement are not available from the corporate environment, some research has been done in the academic environment. Linear, procedural thought patterns measured by programming aptitude tests have been shown to correlate with field-independent learning styles (Foreman, 1988). Although Foreman's study found that field-independence, which is more prevalent in males, was strongly related to programming skills, there is conflicting evidence about whether only field-independent learners will be successful in programming. For example, Dixon (1987) found that there was no significant connection between learning-style preference and programming achievement.

Nevertheless, programming aptitude tests have been used to weed out systematically people with less linear problem-solving styles. Generally, those people are women. The situation is more troubling when we consider that in the pipeline toward information technology jobs programming aptitude tests are used as screening devices for specialized computer training and computer science degree programs. As late as 2001, specialized computer training programs like Hofstra University's Certificate in Computer Science program (Hofstra University, 2001) and George Mason University's Train to Technology Program (George Mason University, 2001) required a high passing grade on a programming aptitude test to enter. In addition, some U.S. programs still require passage of a programming test or a course that covers the same content as a prerequisite for admission to a degree program in computer science (see Utah Valley State College, 2006).

Use of programming aptitude tests as gate-keeping tools for entry into computer training courses at institutions of higher education is problematic in that it filters who can receive advanced computer training. People who have other ways of learning are eliminated from the very programs that would help them understand the requirements for becoming a computer programmer.

As computing environments in business and higher education placed a premium on the skills sets that included linear thinking and single-track problem solving, women became institutionally disconnected from programming training and programming careers in another way, by virtue of their more holistic learning styles.

Access to Technical Education at the High School Level

As the computer age came into full bloom, high schools began to incorporate more rigorous technology training. The late 1950s and the 1960s found U.S. schools engaged in a Cold War competition for technical invention. Science, mathematics, engineering, and fledgling computer science courses became important parts of the high school curriculum.

Public schools dedicated to technology became magnets for the best and brightest technical students. An example of this type of school was Lane Technical High School in Chicago (Lane Tech, n.d.). Originally a public vocational school, Lane responded to a perceived need for scientific and technical expertise by adopting a curriculum rich in scientific and technical content and by instituting selective admissions policy. Although a public high school, Lane Tech never admitted girls, and the new admissions policy continued this tradition. In 1971, Lane Tech became a coeducational facility. Lane Tech's Web site chronicles the move:

> The year 1971 brought the most noticeable change in Lane's history. The Board of Education approved Superintendent James Redmond's recommendation to admit girls to Lane Tech. He cited a drop in enrollment and the lack of a technical school that admits girls, as reasons for the change. The school was in a turmoil after this decision. Fifteen hundred Lane boys protested at the Board of Education. The general fear was that the school's quality would drop and within a few years Lane would be just another high school. Actually, the school's overall academic quality improved with the addition of girls. (Lane Tech, n.d.)

The fact that 1,500 boys walked out of the school rather than attend school with girls shows how deeply ingrained was society's lack of confidence in the technical abilities of girls. Lane Technical High School was not alone in having policies that restricted admission to technical programs to boys (Women's Equity Resource Center, n.d.). But in 1971, schools were legally allowed to restrict their admission by gender. In 1972, things changed.

Title IX

The move to integrate girls into Lane Technical High School's academic program occurred only months before gender discrimination in federally funded institutions was made illegal by the June 23, 1972, passage of Title IX of the Education Amendments of 1972, generally known as Title IX. Although there were some exceptions, Title IX stated that "no person in the United States shall, on the basis of sex, be excluded from participation in, be denied the benefits of, or be subjected to discrimination under any education program or activity receiving Federal financial assistance" (U.S. Department of Labor, Office of Assistant Secretary for Administration and Management, n.d.). If Lane Tech and public schools that received federal funds were legally able to deny admission to girls and young women before Title IX, they were not able to do so afterward.

Although Title IX removed the right of all agencies receiving federal funds to discriminate in educational programs or activities on the basis of sex, the law would still have to be enforced. The U.S. Department of Education's Office for Civil Rights was responsible for enforcement of the law. In 1975, that agency adopted regulations and procedures for enforcement of Title IX. With the passage of time, rules for enforcing Title IX were published by the Departments of Education, Energy, Agriculture, and Health and Human Services. Then on August 30, 2000, comprehensive Title IX rules for 20 federal agencies were enacted (see U.S. Department of Justice, n.d.).

Over 30 years of Title IX enforcement has brought changes in the educational opportunities afforded women. Some change has been won through the courts; other change has been accomplished through voluntary compliance. Girls and women now have the legal right to the same education (at least in federally funded programs) as men. Has this legal right changed the institutional and cultural climate for women seeking technology careers?

The Past Twenty Years

The Current Status

Sadly, removal of legal barriers to educational pathways did not cause an immediate growth in the number of women seeking careers in scientific and technical careers. Although legal pathways to equal educational opportunities had been cleared, institutional barriers still remained. Because women have been systematically excluded from participating, the culture of computing continued to favor male participants. Although nondiscriminatory practices in the workplace have also been illegal since passage of Title VII of the Civil Rights Act of 1964 (Equal Employment Opportunity Commission, n.d.), the perception that computing was "men's work" remained. The male-dominated environment in computing reinforced itself as men continued to find a home in technical programs in universities and industry. Women, on the other hand, were greeted by unwelcoming, hostile spaces that did not value their talent or even their presence. Girls and women encounter several types of disenfranchisement from computing environments. Two of the most prevalent are institutional practices that undervalue the talent of women and environments that promote social isolation of women.

Often extremely talented women are viewed as untalented because of a lack of conformity to the "male" way of doing things. For example, Turkle and Papert (1990) suggest that institutions of higher education, even Harvard, do not always value the ways that women program computers. In talking about the experience of two female students in a programming class at Harvard University, Turkle and Papert note that both students had intellectual styles that were at odds with the top-down structured approach to programming in vogue at Harvard. These female students were nonlinear holistic thinkers. They were uncomfortable with a hierarchical approach.

> [Yet] those who wish to approach the computer in a noncanonical way are discouraged by the dominant computer culture, eloquently expressed in the ideology of the Harvard University course. They are asked to change their style to suit the fashion when they begin to interact with the official computer world, committed to a formal, rule-driven, hierarchical approach to programming. Like Lisa and Robin [the two students], their exclusion from the computer culture is perpetuated not by rules that keep them out, but by ways of thinking that make them reluctant to join in. (p. 135)

The feeling that a woman must change the way she presents her ideas to be accepted in the computing environment is reflected in an interview with Beatrice Fu, director of Microprocessor Software Labs at Intel Corporation in 1997:

> Throughout my career and education, I've been surrounded by white men who have had particular ideas about how things should be done. Many have had their own style, and you're expected to display a similar style to be successful. When I demonstrate what I can do in my own style, I risk not being understood. (Ambrose et al., 1997, p. 183)

It can be a daunting task for any woman to demonstrate competence at her university or in her job, but it is only part of the problem faced by women in male-dominated computing environments. Another important problem is the social isolation and general atmosphere of hostility that women seem to encounter in computer science fields (Ambrose et al., 1997; Cotrell, 1992; Furger, 1998). This atmosphere perpetuates the notion that women do not have ownership of the computing environment and do not belong there.

This feeling of exclusion can start as early as elementary school. Girls and boys can find substantially different environments in the same physical location. For example, in "No Girls Allowed," Melissa Koch (1994) draws a very vivid picture of the difference in treatment of boys and girls in the same computer classroom. Boys are encouraged and validated, while girls are demeaned and marginalized.

This lack of validation for females continues through the university years and into the work environment. Janet Cottrell (1992) notes some of the factors that contribute to the hostile environment for women in computer science. These factors include invisibility—being ignored in the professional setting, patronizing behavior—being "talked down to," and suggestive or obscene behavior. In addition, male-oriented items such as pornographic screen savers often show up in computer labs and add to the feeling that women really do not belong.

Consider the case of Jennifer H. (as cited in Furger, 1998), an accomplished math and science student who chose to study computer science:

> But after her first computer science course—an honors course—at her university, she swore she would never take another class in the department again. Yet it wasn't the work she had trouble with. Jennifer got an A in the class. It was the competitive, macho atmosphere that she wanted no part of. (p. 178)

> "It's like death by a thousand cuts," elaborates one woman I spoke with. "It's lots of little things that all add up to something large. The little comments and attitudes you encounter may not seem like large things, but the fact is that women and minorities deal with these on a daily basis. It all just accumulates." (p. 178)

Dr. Debra Estrin describes facing the same phenomenon as a computer science professor at the University of Southern California. She likens the hostile environment for women to mosquito bites. "When you get just one mosquito bite it's not a problem, but when your body is covered in mosquito bites, you become obsessed with scratching" (interviewed in Ambrose et al., 1997, p. 148).

In spite of these obstacles, women like Estrin continue to pursue careers in computer-related fields And in the past twenty years, girls and women have chosen computer science programs of study and computer-related careers more frequently. However, women continue to be underrepresented all the way down the pathway to computer-related jobs.

In 2000, the AAUW published the landmark report *Tech-Savvy: Educating Girls in the New Computer Age* (2000). The report indicates that one of the reasons that girls do not choose computer-related courses is their perception that such courses will not lead to careers. Based on the culture and the evidence that girls see, they simply do not believe that computer-related careers will be open to them.

Camp (1997) provides a synthesis of the data relating to computer science degrees. Her work indicates that in the academic year 1993–1994, women received 28.7% of the bachelor's degrees, 25.8% of the master's degrees, and 15.4% of the Ph.D. degrees in computer science. Following the pipeline down the academic pathway, women constitute 15.6% of assistant professors, 9.4% of associate professors, and 5.7% of the full professors of computer science.

The picture in the business environment is not much brighter. An analysis of information about workers in high-tech fields reflects the continued underrepresentation of women in these fields. Aggregated data on women programmers, computer scientists, computer engineers, and software designers indicate that women are between 25% and 30% of the total programming work force (U.S. Department of Labor, Women's Bureau, 2002; Information Technology Association of America, 2003). Although data that disaggregate the more technical types of programming from other types of programming are not readily available, women in mid- to upper-level computer engineering jobs in the United States are reported to represent 9% of the total population of computer engineers (Gender Advisory Board, UN Commission on Science and Technology for Development, 1999).

So, thirty years after the passage of Title IX, the percentage of women in senior computing positions hovers below 10% both in business and in academia. If we continue to use the pipeline metaphor, it is clear that the pipeline needs widening. It is equally clear that the leaks in the pipeline need to be patched. This situation begs the question, What is being done to make computing more inclusive and welcoming to girls and women?

Initiatives That Support Women

From the preceding discussion, it is clear that the status of girls and women with reference to computer-related study and careers is complicated. On the one hand, almost all the legal barriers to obtaining training and employment in information technology have been removed. On the other hand, the institutionalization of the male-dominated computing culture has provided barriers that are harder to overcome.

Today, however, there are many initiatives that aim to overcome those barriers and make computing more inclusive and welcoming for females. Among these initiatives are K–12 programs designed to overcome the "men only" image of computing, reformed and reconceptualized university programs aimed at making the academic environment more welcoming, and outreach and mentoring programs, supported by women's professional organizations, intended to provide models of success for girls and women.

K–12 programs. Educators, computer scientists, activists, and others concerned with the status of girls and women have all recognized that widening the pipeline at its inception is a significant strategy for finishing with more computer scientists at the pipeline's end. With this goal in mind, many organizations have implemented programs to get girls involved with computers.

A casual search of the Internet reveals hundreds of programs dedicated to bringing more girls into computing. One example, the Ada Project (n.d.), a clearinghouse for information about girls, women, and computing, lists over thirty organizations that provide support for girls' engagement in technology. These resources include organizations that support girls in the pipeline entry fields (math, science, and engineering) as well as in technology. Also included are organizations that promote careers in technology.

Support for girls entering the pipeline, as well as encouragement to stay in the pipeline, is provided in several ways. Technology clubs, summer camps, and telementoring are some of the direct activities designed to draw girls and young women to technology. In addition, Web sites, books, and exhibitions provide information for girls who are already interested in technology and need ways to sustain that interest.

University reforms. A large study by Margolis and Fisher (2002) was reported in detail in their book *Unlocking the Clubhouse: Women in Computing.* Margolis and Fisher studied women who majored in computer science, interviewing more than 100 students at Carnegie Mellon University. They found that women in the computer science program had a very different experience than men: men and women often came to computer science with different preparation and different expectations, women were turned off by the "geek culture" that requires them to sacrifice a personal life for interaction with the computer, and women felt that the computer culture is an "all-boys" clubhouse. Having determined that the environment in computing was hostile, foreign, and intimidating to many women, Margolis and Fisher made suggestions for changes to the computer culture in Carnegie Mellon University's computer science program. These changes—making adjustments for the level of experience of all students, changing teaching focus to address diverse learners, contextualizing computer science instruction, and transitioning from a "hacker" to a multidimensional approach—increased both the number and retention of female computer science students.

The success that Carnegie Mellon's program has experienced, in both the recruitment and retention of female students, provides hope that Mellon's multidimensional, inclusive program can serve as a model for other computer science programs. Some of the issues raised by the Mellon research have already resulted in changes to computer science programs at the university level. Some examples are department-based programs to increase communication and support among female computer science students, such as the program at University of California at Berkeley (Post-gazett.com, 1999) and the formation of women's computing students organization such as the one at Texas Tech (Aggie Women in Computer Science, n.d.).

Professional organizations. Another interesting development is the increase in mentoring done by women who are successful in computer-related fields. Professional organizations such as Systers, the Computer Research Association's Committee on the Status of Women (CRA-W), and the Association for Computing Machinery's Committee on Women in Computing (ACM-W) have provided support for girls and women seeking careers in computer-related fields. This support has been in the form of lobbying, programs, and general information. The ACM-W Web site (n.d.) describes the organizational purpose this way: "[The ACM-W] celebrates, informs and supports women in computing, and works with the ACM-W community of computer scientists, educators, employers and policy makers to improve working and learning environments for women." A common goal of these organizations is to disrupt the notion that computing and computer-related careers are only for men (CRA-W, n.d.; Systers, n.d.)

The Horizon and Beyond

It would seem that women have every reason to enter computer-based careers. The legal barriers to education and equal employment have been removed. Mentoring organizations have proliferated. Universities have become more aware of the need to restructure their programs. With these things in mind, one might expect that the number of women pursuing careers in computing would have increased geometrically, but this does not seem to be the case. The number of women receiving bachelor's degrees in computer science in 2004 was actually about the same as the number of women receiving the same degree in 1985 (National Science Foundation, 2006). And the percentage of women who graduate with computer science bachelor's degrees has actually declined (National Science Foundation). What, then, is on the horizon for women in computer science?

Educational Opportunities

Although the Title IX legislation of the early 1970s made illegal discrimination by any educational agency that received federal funds, enforcement of Title IX in the areas of technology has been slow. The National Coalition for Women and Girls in Education report *Title IX at 30: Report Card on Gender Equity* (2002) grades the progress toward gender equity in technology as "D" and states,

> The Government has done little to enforce Title IX in the new area of technology. OCR [the U.S. Department of Education's Office for Civil Rights] has apparently conducted no compliance reviews to ensure that girls and women get equal opportunities, although such reviews are sorely needed. OCR needs to make a greater effort to ensure that as educational institutions incorporate technology into their programs and provide more technology opportunities to students, women and girls are not left behind. (p. 54)

Many people see Title IX as the law that equalizes opportunity for girls and women only in athletics. However, Title IX was meant to provide opportunity in all aspects of education. Clearly, that is not happening as quickly as it should.

Although institutions are not changing as quickly as they should to accommodate equal technology opportunities for girls and women, external institutions have stepped in to help recruit girls to the field and widen the pipeline at its inception. As noted earlier, many organizations have developed programs to mentor elementary, middle school, and high school girls and provide inclusive, welcoming experiences in technology. In addition, monies from federal organizations such as the National Science Foundation

(2002) and private corporate foundations such as Dell Foundation (2007) have become available to support technology programs for girls.

Women continue to be underrepresented at every level of postsecondary education. There is some good news, however. From 1995 to 2004, the percentage of women earning master's degrees in computer science has risen from 26.4% to 31.2%, and the percentage of women earning doctorates has increased from 16.5% to 20.5% (National Science Foundation, 2006). In addition, during the same time period, bachelor's degrees in the related entry field of engineering have increased from 17.3% to 20.5% and in the entry field of mathematics have remained close to 50% (46.9% in 1995, 45.9% in 2004).

Careers in Technology

If we accept the premise that the markers of progress toward a computer-related career are (a) interest in computers while in elementary and middle school, (b) completion of computer courses in high school, (c) completion of a computer science (or related) undergraduate degree, and (d) possible completion of postbaccalaureate work in computer science, then there appears to be cause for concern. Clearly, women have not reached the point where they are represented in equal numbers to men at any stage of the journey toward a technical career.

Women's underrepresentation does not appear to be as critical of an issue for business as it is for the academic environment. As noted earlier, almost half of women employed in computer-related fields today received degrees in other areas. On-the-job training can be substituted for academic credentials in the business world. In addition, because Title VII of the Civil Rights Act of 1964, the Age Discrimination in Employment Act of 1967, and the Americans with Disabilities Act of 1990 make it illegal to discriminate in any aspect of employment including recruitment and testing (EEOC, n.d.), the gate-keeping programming aptitude tests have been called into question. Some companies have stopped aptitude testing, and others have become more cautious and aware of pitfalls and prejudices of the tests.

In the academic environment, however, because of the doctoral requirement for computer science faculty members, it is essential that women interested in the professoriate progress through to the pipeline's end. Although their journeys may not be direct, they must be complete. For this reason, women who aspire to careers in the academy find themselves constantly in the minority with no alternative but to persevere or find another career.

Regardless of which computer-related career women choose, they are still likely to find themselves in unwelcoming territory. Because all the legal barriers to computer-related careers have been removed, it is the older, societal and institutional barriers that remain. Just because a woman has the right to have a career in computer science and the education that leads to that career does not mean that she will choose that career.

References

Ada Project. (n.d). Retrieved May 5, 2007, from http://women.cs.cmu.edu/ada/

Aggie Women in Computer Science. (n.d.). Retrieved May 5, 2007, from http://awics.cs.tamu.edu/index.php

Alper, J. (1993). The pipeline is leaking women all the way. *Science, 260*(5106), 409–411.

Ambrose, S., Dunkle, K., Lazarus, B., Nair, I., & Harkus, D. (1997). *Journeys of women in science and engineering: No universal constants.* Philadelphia: Temple University Press.

American Association of University Women. (2000). *Tech-savvy: Educating girls in the computer age.* AAUW Educational Foundation Commission on Technology, Gender, and Teacher Education. Retrieved June 2, 2007, from http://aauw.org/member_center/publications/TechSavvy/TechSavvy.pdf

Association for Computing Machinery's Committee on Women in Computing. (n.d.). Web site home page. Retrieved May 5, 2007, from http://women.acm.org/

Camp, T. (1997). The incredible shrinking pipeline. *Communications of the ACM, 40*(10). Retrieved April 30, 2007, from http://women.acm.org/documents/pipelineshrinkage.htm

Computer Research Association's Committee on the Status of Women. (n.d.). Retrieved May 5, 2007, from http://www.cra.org/Activities/craw/

Costa, N. (1998). *Discussion on human resources online bulletin board.* Retrieved January 13, 2001, from http://www.hronline.com/forums/hrnet/9810/msg00323.html

Cottrell, J. (1992), *I'm a stranger here myself: A consideration of women and computing.* Paper presented at 1992 ACM conference. Retrieved August 6, 2001, from ftp://cpsr.org/cpsr/gender/cottrell.stranger

Dell Foundation. (2007). *The Dell Foundation: Connected communities.* Retrieved May 12, 2007, from http://www.dell.com/content/topics/global.aspx/corp/foundation/en/connectedecomm?c = us&l = en&s = corp

Dixon, V. (1987). *An investigation of prior sources of difficulties in learning university computer science.* Paper presented at the National Educational Computer Conference. (ERIC Document Reproduction Service No. ED295596)

Equal Employment Opportunity Commission. (n.d). *Federal laws prohibiting job discrimination: Questions and answers.* Retrieved May 7, 2007, from http://www.eeoc.gov/facts/qanda.html.

Foreman, K. (1988). *Cognitive style, cognitive ability, and the acquisition of initial computer programming competence.* Paper presented at the annual meeting of the Association for Educational Communications and Technology. (ERIC Document Reproduction Service No. ED 295 638)

Furger, R. (1998). *Does Jane compute? Preserving our daughters' place in the cyber revolution.* New York: Warner Books.

Gender Advisory Board, UN Commission on Science and Technology for Development. (1999). *Gender equity in science and technology.* Retrieved January 4, 2004, from http://gab.wigsat.org/wsis.html

George Mason University. (2001). *George Mason's train to technology program.* Retrieved November 15, 2001, from http://ttt.gmu.edu/prices_adm.htm

Hofstra University. (2001). *Certificate in computer science.* Retrieved November 15, 2001, from http://www.hofstra.edu/academics/ucce/compstu/ucce_compstu_ccs.cfm

Information Technology Association of America. (2003). *Underrepresented groups in the information technology workforce.* Retrieved January 4, 2004, from http://www.itaa.org/workforce/studies/recruit.htm

Jensen, J. (1967). *How to pass computer programmer aptitude tests.* New York: Cowles Education Corporation.

Koch, M. (1994). No girls allowed. *Technos Quarterly, 3*(3). Retrieved August 1, 2001, from http://www.technos.net/journal/volume3/3koch.htm

Koerber, A. (2000). Toward a feminist rhetoric of technology. *Journal of Business and Technical Communication, 14*(1). Retrieved May 29, 2007, from http://www.lib.ncsu.edu:2971/content/vol14/issue1/

Lane Tech. (n.d.). *Lane Tech College Prep—History.* Retrieved April 30, 2007, from http://www.lanetech.org/aboutlanetech.htm

Margolis, J., & Fisher, A. (2002). *Unlocking the clubhouse: Women in computing.* Cambridge, MA: MIT Press.

National Coalition for Women and Girls in Education. (2002). *Title IX at 30: Report card on gender equity.* Retrieved April 30, 2007, from http://www.ncwge.org/PDF/title9at30-6-11.pdf

National Science Foundation. (2002). *NSF's Program for Gender Equity in science, technology, engineering, and mathematics: A brief retrospective 1993–2001.* Retrieved May 10, 2007, from http://www.nsf.gov/pubs/2002/nsf02107/nsf02107.pdf

National Science Foundation. (2006). *Women, minorities, and persons with disabilities in science and engineering.* Retrieved May 5, 2007, from http://www.nsf.gov/statistics/wmpd/sex.html

Oldenziel, R. (1999). *Making technology masculine.* Amsterdam: University of Amsterdam Press.

Otterbein University. (n.d.). *The machine that changed the world.* Retrieved May 5, 2005, from http://www.otterbein.edu/home/fac/dvdjstck/CSC100/CSC100TM TCTW.htm#Gia nt%20B rains

Post-gazette.com. (1999). *CMU's push to put more females in computer science is paying off.* Retrieved May 5, 2007, from http://www.post-gazette.com/regionstate/19990820compwomen4.asp

Spender, D. (1995). *Nattering on the net: Women, power and cyberspace.* North Melbourne, Australia: Spinifex.

Stanley, A. (1992). Do mothers invent? The feminist debate in history of technology. In C. Kramarae & D. Spender (Eds.), *The knowledge explosion: Generations of feminist scholarship.* New York: Teachers College Press.

Stanley, A. (1993). *Mothers and daughters of invention: Notes for a revised history of technology.* Metuchen, NJ: Scarecrow Press.

Systers. (n.d). Retrieved May 5, 2007, from http://www.systers.org

Turkle, S., & Papert, S. (1990). Epistemological pluralism: Styles and voices within the computer culture. *Signs, 16*(1), 128–157.

Turner, S., Bernt, P., & Pedora, N. (2002). *Why women choose information technology careers: Educational, social and familial influences.* Paper presented at the annual meeting of the American Educational Research Association, 2002. (ERIC Document Reproduction Service No. ED465878)

U.S. Department of Justice. (n.d.). *Title IX Legal Manual.* Retrieved on May 5, 2007, from http://www.usdoj.gov/crt/cor/coord/ixlegal.htm

U.S. Department of Labor, Office of Assistant Secretary for Administration and Management. (n.d.). *Title IX, Education Amendments of 1972,* sec. 168(a). Retrieved on April 30, 2007, from http://www.dol.gov/oasam/regs/statutes/titleix.htm

U.S. Department of Labor, Women's Bureau. (2002). *Women in high-tech jobs.* Retrieved on January 4, 2004, from http://www.dol.gov/wb/factsheets/hitech 02.htm

Utah Valley State College. (2006). *Utah Valley State College—advising sheet.* Retrieved on April 20, 2007, from http://www.utahsbr.edu/Agendas/2006_Agendas/Mar102006.pdf

Women's Equity Resource Center. (n.d.). *Resources to infuse equity: Report card—career education.* Retrieved April 30, 2007, from http://www2.edc.org/WomensEquity/resource/title9/report/career.htm

Woodfield, R. (2000). *Women, work and computing.* Cambridge, UK: Cambridge University Press.

Zierdt-Warshaw, L., Winkler, A., & Bernstein, L. (2000). *American women in technology: An encyclopedia.* Santa Barbara, CA: ABC-CLIO.

5

HELPING WOMEN IMPROVE STATISTICS LEARNING ONLINE THROUGH AUTHENTIC LEARNING AND EMOTIONAL INTELLIGENCE

Marilyn K. Simon

Why do so many people think statistics is sadistic? In my opinion the reason for this is due to a fear of mathematics. Statistics involves using mathematical techniques to understand number relationships. The student has to know what technique to apply in order to achieve the expected result. This fear can be a product of many things. Students usually grow up studying this subject. The first things taught are usually reading and math right from the beginning. The fear of math is not in a person's genes nor is it hereditary, but I was told that the ability to do math is innate. I was told early on that as a female I would always struggle with math.

—M.B.A. student in managerial statistics

This student's response illustrates many women's, and men's, perception of studying quantitative and scientific fields. In early 2005, Dr. Lawrence H. Summers, the president of Harvard, gave a keynote address at a conference for women and science. During his speech, Summers posited that people who are worried about the relative dearth of women in the upper ranks of science should consider the possibility that women simply cannot *hack it*, that their genes or the wiring of their brains leave them less fit than men for math and, therefore, for science. People who support Summers's proposition point out that in the past two decades there has been a substantial increase in the opportunities, training, and encouragement given to girls and women to improve their mathematical performance and foster greater involvement in math-related fields and that the barriers to women entering these careers have thus been removed. Therefore one should look for innate reasons for the lack of women in mathematically related fields.

Although there has been progress made in the number of women who choose to major in and obtain bachelor's degrees in mathematics or the natural and physical sciences, the number of women majoring in other math-related disciplines such as engineering and computer science pales in comparison to the number of their male colleagues (National Center for Education Statistics [NCES], 2003). Women make up 42% of all science majors, but most are found in the fields of biology, molecular biophysics, and biochemistry. Women are also underrepresented in several mathematics-heavy social science disciplines, such as economics, in which only 26% of majors are women.

The argument by Summers and others that each sex has its own unique sphere of excellence, with mathematics falling "naturally" into men's domain, does not coincide with measures of assessment of the mathematical abilities of children. Since 1960, the National Assessment of Educational Progress (NAEP) has been publishing the results regarding the differences between males and females in mathematics. NAEP studies (NCES, 1994, 1997, 2000, 2003) found that at ages 9 and 13 girls score slightly higher than boys in math proficiency tests, which include visualization skills, but by age 17 girls start to lag behind boys. This difference, however, is only 1%. The 1997 NAEP study revealed that female seniors were more likely than male seniors to say that they did not take additional mathematics because of poor performance in the subject matter, despite the fact that there were no significant differences between their achievement and that of their male cohorts. It appears from the NAEP studies that women are not innately inferior to males in mathematical ability or talents, but as females move through the educational system they begin to doubt their mathematical abilities and fail to enhance their skills. Fausto-Sterling (1992) conducted a meta-analysis of gender difference in mathematical ability and found that all differences could be explained by socialization rather than biology.

What Summers failed to mention in his speech, and what the statistics do not reveal, is that women continue to suffer affronts and disadvantages—including ridicule in middle school math and science classes, benign neglect in high school, and, later on, problems with access to higher education due to the lack of availability of adequate child care and higher levels of domestic responsibilities—to a much greater degree than their male cohorts. After 10 or more years, these affronts can add up to real barriers. People who wish to determine if the relative lack of women in the upper reaches of science is chromosome based should give close attention to the social inequities beginning in the middle school years. Once these biases are eliminated, maybe then we would have a better understanding of the gender gap in math and science.

Another area that needs to be understood is the role that parents play in their children's self-perceptions. In two longitudinal studies of school-age children and their parents, Eccles, Jacobs, and Harold (1990) found that parents generally tend to make stereotypic attributions for their sons' and daughters' math performance, and these attributions are negatively related to their daughters' self-perceptions and decisions to engage in math-related activities. These findings were similarly documented in later research (Jacobs & Weisz, 1994; Tiedemann, 2000). Such findings could shed light on the ways in which girls might be socialized to see themselves as being poor in math from an early age.

Why Is It Important for Female Students to Succeed in Math and Statistics?

As long as women are marginalized in physics, economics, engineering, and many areas of mathematics, they will not be able to play a significant role in developing new technologies or deciding how these technologies are to be put to use. Women's marginalization in these fields, in essence, diminishes the power and responsibility of women to enact social change. Furthermore, without role models, many young women are dissuaded from entering careers that have excellent potential (Simon, 2000). The breadth and applicability of mathematics is immense. Mathematics is fundamental not only to science and technology but also to almost all situations that require an analytical model-building approach, whatever the discipline. Mathematics lies behind computer technology, underpins medical technology, and enables space exploration.

Statistics (a most maligned subject) plays a major and increasing role in personal and public life, particularly in medicine, computer science, engineering, quality control, and management, as well as in all areas of physical and social sciences, business, and economics. Statistics is applied anywhere that informed decisions are needed from limited data, and its extensive use has benefited from the substantial advances in computing powers. Advances in public policy are made possible through the application of statistical techniques.

Changes in technology have altered higher education in unforeseen ways. Many women now access higher education through online or distance learning courses, a venue that carries different challenges than face-to-face instruction. Many women enter these degree programs with the hope of advanced employment, and they thus need to succeed in math and statistics in order to obtain their degree. Although behaviors as complex as career choice are multidetermined phenomena, without a solid foundation in mathematics and statistics many important, high-paying, and influential fields are closed to people who are fearful and ill prepared in mathematics and statistics.

Teaching Statistics Online

Kramarae (2001) conducted a study for the American Association of University Women (AAUW) and found that distance, or online, learning was on the rise and that women make up the majority of online students. Of these nontraditional online learners, 60% are over 25 years old and female. I have been fortunate in my 30-plus years as a mathematics educator to teach statistics to thousands of students, on the ground, online, and in secondary, undergraduate, and graduate institutions. Most of my female students have one characteristic in common: they have significant levels of mathematics anxiety, which translates into a fear and dread of statistics. Moreover, their student colleagues have informed them that statistics is *sadistic,* reinforcing their fear. The problem is compounded for women because traditional cultural stereotypes support the notion that mathematics (and therefore statistics) is a man's subject.

Teaching statistics in an online environment adds extra challenges, beyond those of traditional facilitation, for female students and their instructors. Having generally been acculturated differently from men, women often bring a different set of perspectives into their learning environment and are more likely to have a perceived need for face-to-face contact, hand-holding, and personal interaction (Simon, 2000). These challenges can be overwhelming for students and might help explain the high attrition rate of female students taking statistics, and other "tough" courses, online. In an online learning environment in which instructors and students cannot see one another, the ability to read the emotions of others, and offer appropriate feedback and support quickly, is an important factor for success.

The annual dropout rate for first-year students who seek traditional postsecondary degrees in the United States is approximately 14% (Flood, 2002). Lynch (2001) determined that the dropout rate rises to between 35% and 50% (depending on the online program) for students who are in distance learning programs in which face-to-face meetings between learners and instructors are rare and communication is primarily through asynchronous, computer-mediated means. Without extra support and motivation, the chances for student success are diminished.

Online education fulfills a need for students who cannot attend traditional classrooms. Single working mothers, in particular, find online learning the only means of furthering their education and increasing their job opportunities. Most online courses are also accelerated courses that are adult friendly and provide a focused, logical path to a degree. In the past, there may have been little or no time for busy people to attend college. Now, they can set their own schedule and not have to leave their family to attend classes. At the same time, online learning offers them the ability to increase skills, improve the chances of finding a higher paying job, improve living situations, make outside contacts and network with other adults, and set a positive example for their children by teaching them that learning and achieving is an ongoing process. Drucker (1992) posited, "It is a safe prediction that in the next fifty years schools and universities will change more and more drastically than they have since they assumed their present form 300 years ago when they organized themselves around the printed book" (p. 97). Online learning is already actualizing Drucker's prophecy. Anderson and

Haddad (2005) found that women fare well in the online course environments, when provided with opportunities for self-expression and when their emotional needs are met.

The benefits of online and distance learning support the need for more research into best practices using this medium. This approach to postsecondary education, however, still requires that students master a variety of disciplines, including mathematics and statistics.

Mathphobia

In the United States, math anxiety (also known as mathphobia) appears to be quite prevalent. It is believed that 87% of the adult female population suffers from some form of mathematics anxiety, which often shows up as math avoidance and then math incompetence (Tobias, 1980). There are many reasons why this condition exists, one being that many people think that mathematics is the art of computing and that mathematicians spend all their time making advanced calculations. If art appreciation were taught in the same way that mathematics is, it would consist of learning how to mix paints.

The study of statistics invokes the same feelings of inadequacy and panic in students. As a teacher of statistics, and usually online statistics, I have found that students express this sense of anxiety explicitly. In an MBA program, I asked the following question of female students enrolled in an online quantitative analysis course in March 2004: Why do people think statistics is sadistic?

One woman expressed the idea that math anxiety and literacy are socially constructed, accepted, and even perhaps encouraged in women:

> I can attest that I am one of those people who think statistics is sadistic! Any form of math to me is a problem and a nightmare. It's the typical response that what you don't know scares you. We live in a country that is mathematically illiterate, so anything involving math is going to be considered "sadistic." When growing up, I was told that as a female, I would not have much need for math. I now realize that was the worst message I could have received.

This woman expressed the idea of "not needing math," and even though statistical information is now such a large part of adult life, this view of uselessness seems to remain.

It appears that students sense that learning statistics will automatically be difficult and require an extensive amount of work, perhaps more than in other disciplines:

> Why do so many people think statistics is sadistic? Sadistic means extremely cruel. There is a myth among the math world that statistics is a lot of numbers all running together performing different functions. After you have all the data it's hard to interpret their use. Statistics to a certain level is cruel if a student is not applying themselves properly. This is a serious course that performs a lot of functions and I think it's hard work and people always assume the worst for some reason. Now that I'm in the course I can see it's like almost any other course—you will achieve if you apply yourself and utilize your resources to achieve success.

This woman suggested that the myths of despair surrounding mathematics and statistics actually exceed the reality of succeeding in these courses. Her statement suggests that the ways in which math and statistics are taught early in students' schooling might determine the perception of quantitative courses for the duration of their studies. In fact, the personality and teaching style of the professor may determine a student's success more than any other factor, as noted by another female student:

> I think a lot of people are intimidated by math in general. Perhaps in high school algebra or college calculus, the average student has had a bad experience with math. In particular, many students, especially female students, have a problem with statistics because it involves critical thinking versus simple arithmetic. With statistics, one must be able to analyze data and determine what the results mean. If you can't break the results down, then you will be unable to properly interpret the data. When people see all those graphs, numbers, and z-scores, they become intimidated by it (well I do anyway). Then in my own personal experience, my statistics professor in undergrad was not patient with the students who learned slower than others. As a result, I developed a dislike of stats because I could not understand what I was looking at.

Many of the women I questioned have been convinced that they lack the ability to understand mathematics and statistics, almost as if this had been inherited. The following learner explained her own anxiety in a way that suggests that she accepted the fact that she had an innate disability when it came to learning math:

> Stats can be a foreign concept to those who are mathematically impaired like me. I think that people feel this way because statistics is a scary thing when you are not good at math and you have to try to figure out how to get the statistical information you need. I read somewhere that for many companies, statistics seem like sadistic because the information that results from analyses is impossible for so many to interpret. This could be one of the factors affecting the sticky floor or the glass ceiling for female executives.

This woman's statement implies that a seemingly inherited lack of ability in quantitative fields might explain the barriers to women's success in many fields, but it is not apparent that she viewed a way out of this quagmire.

The following quotation revealed the severity of math anxiety that can be felt by students. This woman described a level of fear that seemed to consume her, resulting in difficulties in other facets of her life. However, she ended her statement by noting that receiving assistance in a patient manner had kept her from abandoning her studies.

> I have always steered clear away from math or anything to do with math, like this class. I have learned much about numerical information in this online class. I have been challenged almost beyond my point of sanity. I clearly see in myself high levels of anxiety. This has effects on my family, work, and social life. Without the help and understanding I received here, I would have dropped this class within the first week.

All these responses support the notion that there is a general dread of taking statistics and that statistics instructors need to help their students overcome their fears of and resistance to math before any other educational objective can be achieved. The important thread in all these statements, though, suggests that appropriate pedagogy and support can enable students to overcome these fears and succeed in math and statistics. In addition, the perception of a lack of usefulness and relevance of mathematics and statistics is also a deterrent to the study of quantitative fields. Two ideas that hold promise for assisting students in their studies are affective learning and authentic learning.

Emotional Intelligence and the Affective Domain of Learning

Fillip (2002) found that men tend to view distance education primarily as a way to gain access to education across vast distances, whereas women tend to view distance education primarily as a way to connect with people and work toward a common agenda. In an online learning environment in which instructors cannot see students (and vice versa), the ability to read the emotions of others is an important factor for success, especially among female students. Emotional intelligence in a classroom, as described by Cherniss and Goleman (2001), becomes apparent when studying how the instructor manages the classroom, shares responsibility with students for the learning process, empathizes with students' concerns, and builds a collaborative learning experience based on the diverse backgrounds and knowledge of the students. Emotional intelligence is closely tied to the *affective domain* of learning. The affective domain "contains skills that deal with emotions, feelings, and values" (Pacific Crest, 2007, p. 9) and consists of holding and directing students' attention, active participation, values, attitudes and concepts, organization, and behavioral characteristics (Krathwohl, Bloom, & Masia, 1998). Keeping students' attention, assuaging their concerns, and encouraging their active participation are key factors to help set the stage for the success of female students in learning statistics online. Because so many students, especially female students, enter a statistics classroom with a fear of mathematics, it is imperative to acknowledge and address directly the roots and consequences of mathphobia and to offer solutions for a cure.

Applying Affective and Authentic Learning to Online Statistics

Onwuegbuzie and Wilson (2003) determined that statistics anxiety is a debilitative phenomenon. In their Anxiety-Expectation Mediation (AEM) model, they used path analytical techniques to explain how statistics anxiety and expectation play a central role in students' ability to learn. They concluded that statistics teachers need a well-thought-out plan to help their students overcome this malady. The statements by the women learners in my MBA class validate these results.

Research suggests that levels of math and statistics anxiety warrant further attention to the emotional factors involved in cognition, or the affective component of learning. *The Dimensions of Learning*, as originally prepared by the Association for Supervision and Curriculum Development (ASCD, 1991), addressed the importance of emotional intelligence and the affective domain in learning for female learners. When teachers promote their own positive attitudes and perceptions in the learning environment, female students learn more effectively and are more motivated to achieve in the class. As noted in the revised framework of the dimensions of learning (ASCD, 1995), there are five key methods that educators in any learning environment can use to ensure that all students experience positive attitudes and perceptions about the learning process. These methods are especially important to female learners. To enjoy learning, students must do the following:

1. Feel accepted by teachers and peers
2. Experience a sense of comfort and order
3. Perceive tasks as valuable and interesting
4. Believe they have the ability and resources to complete tasks successfully
5. Understand and be clear about tasks, including what they are expected to do, how they are expected to do it, and how they will be evaluated. (ASCD, 1995, p. 1)

The *Dimensions of Learning* also addressed the importance of deep learning, rather than rote memory, in coursework. Helping students acquire and integrate new knowledge is an important aspect of learning. When students are learning new information, they can be guided in relating the new knowledge to what they already know, organizing that information, and then making it part of their long-term memory. When students are acquiring new skills and processes, they can learn a model (or set of steps) and then shape the skill or process to make it efficient and effective for them, and, finally, they can internalize or practice the skill or process so they can perform it easily.

Discussion Questions and Guidelines

Discussions engage students in joint problem solving. Bracewell, Breuleux, Laferriere, Benoit, and Abdous (1998) note that the professional educator should facilitate and guide inquiry-based learning with a collaboration of knowledge building while engaging learners in tasks to interact with other students to alleviate misconceptions and develop the deeper meaning of the subject matter to the task at hand. This method also supports the idea that learners, and especially women learners, need to feel a sense of trust and acknowledgment from their peers.

Smith (1999) advises that "the task of the educator is to work with people so that they may address the initial situation—to move beyond simply knowing that 'something happened' into some sort of *understanding* what the situation means." This kind of development is further enhanced in an online learning environment. In online classes, especially those at a graduate level, it is expected that the majority of the interactions will be among students; however, the facilitator should assume a nudging and guiding role in the discussions as needed and aim to contribute something of value each day. The facilitator should also make certain that discussions are not dominated by any particular member or group. In most online courses, discussion questions posted each week are designed to be open-ended and elicit critical and creative thoughts. In addition, the use of reflective journals can contribute to an enhanced online learning experience, allowing students to place the content and the process into their own framework by using their own words and thoughts.

Reflective Journal or Summaries

Reflective thinking helps students approach their learning in a thoughtful manner and deal more effectively with a field characterized by uncertainty, complexity, and variety. In the online statistics courses that I facilitate, learners are asked, each week, to reflect on the three domains of learning—cognitive, affective, and conative, as described in the following list—and to inform the instructor what she can do to assist the learner. Using this three-faceted approach, students are encouraged to integrate the content, the emotions involved in studying statistics, and the process and behaviors required for them to master the coursework.

> *Cognitive*: What did you learn about research and statistics this week that you did not know prior to the course? Summarize the important topics in the course that were discussed this week that were not known to you last week.
>
> *Affective*: What are your feelings about the course, pace, group work, and your participation? How is this course working for you?

Conative: How did you approach the work? What type of input did you put into the material, lessons, discussion, etc.? Discuss any false starts that you might have had. How can your job or profession benefit from what you have learned?

Because I understand the importance of the pedagogy and perception of the instructor's attitude about students, I also ask the following question to enable learners to feel more strongly connected to me and to provide me with the ability to address their personal learning concerns: "What can I do, as an instructor, to ensure that this class is working for you? What do you expect in an instructor that I am or I am not doing? Please be honest! I promise you that it will only be used to make this class better for you and improve my rating :)."

Authentic Projects

Learning does not stop with acquiring and integrating knowledge. Learners need to develop an in-depth understanding through the process of extending and refining and applying the knowledge (e.g., by making new distinctions, clearing up misconceptions, and reaching conclusions). Arguably, the most effective learning occurs when knowledge is utilized to perform meaningful tasks. Thus, I require students in my online statistics course to create a research project, related to their chosen profession, in which primary data are collected and analyzed.

Wlodkowski (1999) posits that authentic performance tasks are one of the oldest forms of assessment and should be a staple in the adult-learning classroom. The closer that assessment procedures come to allowing learners to demonstrate what they have learned in the environment in which they will eventually use that learning, the greater will be the learners' motivation to do well and the more they can understand their competence and feel the self-confidence that emerges from effective performance. Authentic learning implies that learners should apply their knowledge to the real world. When applying research and statistics, they should think like a researcher and statistician.

As fears begin to subside through the use of multiple methods of support and reassurance, and as students become more comfortable with quantitative information, the discussion questions can take on a more authentic tone. For example, answering the following questions can help students search for bona fide uses of statistics: "What problem in your profession or personal life could lead to testing a hypothesis that would employ a t-test (chi-square, ANOVA, etc.)?" and "Explain what types of data would need to be collected and how the data would be analyzed to test a specific hypothesis and solve the problem posed."

To keep discussions flowing, students are required to respond to their colleagues with (a) a challenging question requiring further research, (b) additional information that allows the original material to be understood in a new light, or (c) a new synthesis of material already presented allowing another interpretation. Addressing the fears first, allowing feelings of success, and then using authentic projects appears to address the two main barriers exhibited in the students' comments: anxiety when studying statistics and the perceived uselessness of mathematics and statistics in everyday life.

Conclusion

If an online facilitator is able to understand the students, and provide them with the tools necessary to overcome their perceived barriers to learning, success is likely. Perceptions, attitudes, and beliefs are brought into any classroom environment, regardless of the medium used. In an online statistics classroom, using authentic learning, addressing emotional intelligence, providing students with tools to help eliminate mathematics anxiety, and facilitating the acquisition of new knowledge are critical not only to enlist students to interact but also to help students overcome their fears and keep them interested, motivated, and moving toward success in statistics. Statistics anxiety is a real and prevalent experience that is experienced by the majority of female students in postsecondary education. An unpleasant experience in a statistics class can keep some individuals from pursuing certain career paths in the decision-making fields. It is important for a facilitator to implement strategies to ensure equal access to all classes for men and women. In addition, statistics educators need to be sensitive to the variability in their students' skills in and attitudes toward mathematics and to remove the notion that statistics is sadistic.

References

Anderson, D. M., & Haddad, C. J. (2005). Gender, voice and learning in online course environments. *Journal of Asynchronous Learning Networks, 9*(1), 1–16.

Association for Supervision and Curriculum Development (ASCD). (1991, 1995). *Dimensions of learning: Reflecting on positive attitudes and perceptions about learning.* Retrieved August 15, 2002, from http://webserver2.ascd.org

Bracewell, R., Breuleux, A., Laferriere, T., Benoit, J., & Abdous, M. (1998). *The emerging contribution of online resources and tools to classroom learning and teaching.* Vancouver, Canada: TeleLearning Network. Retrieved October 8, 2003, from http://www.tact.fse.ulaval.ca/ang/html/review98.html#anchor434429

Cherniss, C., & Goleman, D. (2001). *The emotionally intelligent workplace: How to select for, measure, and improve emotional intelligence in individuals, groups, and organizations.* San Francisco: Jossey-Bass.

Drucker, P. T. (1992). *Managing for the future: The 1990s and beyond.* New York: Penguin.

Eccles, J., Jacobs, J., & Harold, R. (1990). Gender role stereotypes, expectancy effects, and parents' socialization of gender differences. *Journal of Social Issues, 46,* 183–201.

Fausto-Sterling, A. (1992). *Myths of gender: Biological theories about women and men.* New York: Basic Books.

Fillip, B. (2002). *Reality check: Actors and emerging knowledge networks in the South.* October 2002 Reader for the Crystal eLearning Symposium.

Flood, J. (2002). Read all about it: Online learning facing 80% attrition rates. *Turkish Online Journal of Distance Education, 3*(2). Retrieved March 1, 2004, from http://tojde.anadolu.edu.tr/tojde6/articles/jim2.htm

Jacobs, J. E., & Weisz, V. (1994). Gender stereotypes: Implications for gifted education. *Roeper Review, 6,* 152–155.

Kramarae, C. (2001). *The third shift: Women learning online.* American Association of University Women. Retrieved June 17, 2006, from http://www.aauw.org/research/3rdshift.cfm

Krathwohl, D., Bloom, B., & Masia, B. (1998). Taxonomy of educational objectives, handbook II: Affective domain. In F. Schultz (Ed.), *SOURCES: Notable selections in education* (2nd ed., p. 271). Guilford, CT: McGraw-Hill.

Lynch, M. M. (2001, November/December). Effective student preparation for online learning. *Technology Source.* Retrieved September 8, 2002, from http://ts.mivu.org/default.asp?show=article&id=901

National Center for Education Statistics (NCES). (1994, 1997, 2000, 2003). *NAEP: Trends in Academic Progress* (NCES 97–095). Washington, DC: U.S. Department of Education.

Onwuegbuzie, A., & Wilson, V. (2003). Statistics anxiety: nature, etiology, antecedents, effects, and treatments—a comprehensive review of literature. *Teaching in Higher Education, 8*(2), 195–210.

Pacific Crest. (2007). *Introduction to process education.* Retrieved June 14, 2008, from http://www.pcrest.com/PE/PE3.htm

Simon, M. (2000). *The evolution of women in mathematics.* Reston, VA: NCTM.

Smith, M. (1999). *Experience: Is there a difference between "having an experience" and "knowing an experience"?* Retrieved December 8, 2003, from http://www.infed.org/biblio/b-exper.htm

Tiedemann, J. (2000). Parents' gender stereotypes and teachers' beliefs as predictors of children's concept of their mathematical ability in elementary school. *Journal of Educational Psychology, 92,* 144–151.

Tobias, S. (1980, September/October). Math anxiety: What you can do about it. *Today's Education,* 26GS–29GS.

Wlodkowski, R. (1999). *Enhancing adult motivation to learn.* San Francisco: Jossey-Bass.

6

EXAMINING THE BAGGAGE

First Steps Toward Transforming Habits of Mind Around Race in Higher Education

Crystal Gafford Muhammad and Adrienne D. Dixson

Bag lady you gone hurt your back
Dragging all them bags like that
I guess nobody ever told you
All you must hold on to
Is you, is you, is you . . .
So pack light

—Erykah Badu, "Bag Lady" (2000)

In an age of politically correct color blindness, it is important that higher education engage students in honest discourse about diversity (King, 1991). Throughout higher education, most faculty as well as students regard themselves as multiculturally aware, without regard for varying degrees of multicultural competence (Bennett & Bennett, 2004; King, 1991). Transforming perspectives related to race and other diversities requires students to become aware of their identities, influences that have shaped those identities, and their attendant habits of mind and ways of being around matters of diversity (Sheared, 1994). What does it take to foster openness to questioning previously unexamined and unquestioned perspectives in order to consider alternative perspectives on race?

If our students believe that they are multiculturally aware but in actuality are only politically correct, then merely assigning readings and lecturing about the salience of race perpetuates superficial attention to race and racism in education (King, 1991; Kolb, 1984). Thus, we must shift from acknowledging the bags that women bring to unpacking them to create awareness of racial distortions that they may not realize they are carrying. Of particular import for this discussion is the notion of multicultural competence and the varying degrees of multicultural competence across diversity factors. More directly, just because women students may have multicultural competence around issues of gender, this competence does not necessarily translate into competence around race. However, a bridge between these intersecting identities can be forged in order to translate empathetic understanding in one context to sympathetic engagement in another.

Theoretically speaking, this chapter draws on the work of Kathleen Taylor (2000), focusing on teaching with the intention of developing critical awareness about race. It is our basic premise that we cannot get past race and racism in our classroom environments until we first take account of how race influences our lives (Blackmun, 1978; Essed, 1991). In this vein, our work fuses the psychological theories of Nigrescence (Cross & Fhagen-Smith, 2001) and White racial identity development (Hardiman, 2001) with transformative learning theory (Mezirow, 2000), while specifically focusing on women learners (Collins, 2000; Hayes & Flannery, 2000). On the side of transformative learning theory, this bridge is anchored in Mezirow's idea that transformative learning cannot begin until a person arrives at a "disorienting dilemma" or triggering event (2000). On the side of racial identity development, a racial encounter experience is necessary to foster growth (Cross & Fhagen-Smith, 2001; Hardiman, 2001). In merging theory with practice, we as educators can create the "disorienting dilemma"/triggering encounter, enabling students to review critically their bags in order to connect their book knowledge about race with their habits of mind (Taylor, 2000). The goal, in lyricist Erykah Badu's terms, is to enable students to "pack light" around issues of race. This goal that we have for our students is particularly relevant when our students are educators: The bags that educators carry influence the education of generations to come (hooks, 1981/1995).

This chapter begins with a short narrative and discussion of the intersectionality of race and gender in the classroom. As the title of this volume acknowledges, women students are in the numerical majority. Even if this numerical majority were empowered on campus, however, that majoritarian power would not necessarily be held by women of color, as campus cultures are not only androcentric but also Eurocentric (Rankin & Reason, 2005). We then enter a theoretical discussion of the intersection between the "disorienting dilemmas"/triggering events of transformative learning theory and the encounter experience necessary to foster racial identity development. From there we engage Taylor's (2000) idea of teaching with developmental intention, addressing the benefits of experiential learning in the development of cultural awareness.

We demonstrate how, using experiential learning techniques, we created a triggering event to jump-start processes of racial identity development and transformative learning in our women students. We detail our method of inquiry, presenting analysis of the written reflections of women in our combined class as they engaged in an experiential learning exercise designed to activate awareness of White privilege (McIntosh, 1998). We find that the employment of this exercise creates a triggering event for women, both Black and White. Psychologically, the women become poised to cycle or recycle through their racial identity development. In terms of transformative learning, the women take critical first steps toward transforming their habits of mind and ways of being about race.

Race and Gender on Campus

During one of the many *Brown v. Board of Education* 50th-anniversary celebrations, Elaine Jones, retired director-counsel for the NAACP Legal Defense Fund, was asked what it was like to be the first Black woman student at the University of Virginia School of Law. In particular, the audience participant wanted to know whether Jones could determine if any of her negative encounters in school could be attributable to race bias or gender bias. Jones answered plainly: it did not matter. Who cared if the chill of the cold campus climate, the insensitivities and indignities experienced, could be traced to her race or gender? It was happening to her!

Fortunately for the purposes of this discussion, Jones did elaborate on her story. She was the only African American in her class, but there were several White women who entered the law school at the same time that she did. After class, the women would meet in the ladies' room and debrief one another on the day's events. As Jones did not know an African American man at the school with whom she could compare stories, she sorted her experiences through the ladies' room debriefings. Although the other women shared their experiences, there were probably experiences that had racial underpinnings that they did not share. What this story underscores is that Jones's knapsack held some common items that women in general carry. She could find empathy over gender matters the same way that one woman will pass a tampon to any woman in need in the next stall. Because of her race, though, Jones's knapsack included other measures and tactics to help her manage and process schoolhouse hostilities that she encountered because of her race.

Arthur Cohen, a scholar in the history of higher education, notes that not much has changed on campuses since the importation of the Cambridge and Oxford model, as embodied by the founding of Harvard College (Cohen, 1998). The implication of Cohen's observation is that although nearly 57 percent of the 16,611,700 undergraduate and graduate students enrolled in U.S. colleges and universities in the fall of 2002 were women (U.S. Department of Education, 2004), campus environments generally remain androcentric, reflective of male cultural customs, norms, and mores (Rankin & Reason, 2005; Swim, Hyers, Cohen, & Ferguson, 2001).

Given the dynamics of the proportion of women students on campus and the male-centeredness of most campus environments, individual culture clashes are inevitable. The degree of culture clash, however, will vary by campus and by individual. Individual personality factors are significant in how an individual woman experiences campus, yet there are sets of challenges that arise from differences across racial, ethnic, class, and sexual orientation lines. Not only are campus environments male centered, but they also tend to privilege the Euro-American, middle- to upper-class heterosexual. People on campus who are neither male, White, middle to upper class, nor heterosexual are least likely to find cultural affinity or feel culturally safe on campus. This chapter focuses solely on differences in perspectives on societal racial dynamics between women in the classroom, in the most simplistic terms—Black and White.

The presence of women of color on campus is nontrivial: 2,903,300 of students enrolled in postsecondary education in 2002, almost one-third of all women (U.S. Department of Education, 2004). Some of the experiences of women students of color mirror those of their White counterparts, but some of their experiences are unique to people of color.

In *How Minority Students Experience College*, Watson, Terrell, Wright, and Associates (2002) report that for many "minority" students, the collegiate environment is mentally unhealthy and contributes to difficulty succeeding academically and developing socially. Although most students of color do not begin college with the notion that racial differences are a concern, they often find that their local K–12 environments inadequately prepared them for college-level work and failed to transmit appropriate social and cultural capital necessary to navigate college campuses. In addition, many students of color find campus environments unwelcoming. One student reports being asked, quite bluntly, by a professor, "What is a Black girl from Detroit doing in an economics class?" and was later asked by the same professor, "Do you ever wonder if you're here because of affirmative action?" (Watson et al., 2002, p. 76). Unfortunately, this student's experience is not isolated, and such experiences can be pervasive on some campuses.

Moreover, students of color report being overlooked in campus discussions, unless the topic is in relation to people of color. In such a context, they are often viewed as the resident spokesperson for their representative group. Would a White student be asked to speak for his or her race? (Watson et al., 2002)

Furthermore, as administrators seem to equate propensity for success with test scores, students of color feel that that there is a lack of understanding, as well as a dearth of academic and emotional support. In fact, Watson et al. (2002) state that "the most significant element influencing the performance level of many students is their inability to connect to an institutional agent" (p. 78). This latter consideration is especially poignant for those students who are neither White nor male. For example, one student in Watson et al.'s study specifically commented, "If you're lucky enough to be a woman of color then you don't have anything, you can't go to anybody on this campus" (p. 60). Hence, when factors of race and ethnicity are taken into consideration, White women on campus have privileges that women of color do not.

The issue and challenge in teaching women to understand race is to get them to consider matters of race beyond understandings of one's individual lack of privilege on certain multicultural line items in order to be able to engage and respect the struggles of others with different sets of privileges. Herein is the foundation of multicultural competence, a fundamental skill set necessary for successfully engaging a pluralistic, democratic society.

Transforming Habits of Mind Around Race: Merging Transformative Learning Theory and Racial Identity Development

Transforming habits of mind around race necessarily implicates racial identity development. The bags that students bring to higher education, the tools and burdens of life acquired, are "polyrhythmic," varying by their familial, work, and educational experiences, as well as by race, class, and gender dynamics (Sheared, 1994). This acquisition of knowledge over one's lifetime remains packed until discarded as no longer useful, no longer reflective of the world as an individual knows it. With respect to understandings of race, models of racial identity development and the accompanying research suggests that people do not grow in their racial perspectives unless their views are challenged.[1] Our suggestion here is that students will not learn about race until a disorienting dilemma or triggering event challenges them to do so.

Models of monoracial identity development are generally centered in the context of interracial contact, often, but not necessarily, negative. These models also generally present three phases of contact: preencounter, encounter, and postencounter (Wijeyesinghe & Jackson, 2001). During the preencounter phase, people are generally unaware of the influence of race, and it is not until an encounter experience—or in transformative learning terms, a disorienting dilemma/triggering event—with someone of a different race that a self-appraisal regarding the meaning of race is made. During the postencounter phase, a person can choose to accept and integrate or reject and deny new knowledge about race. Choices to accept and integrate new knowledge about race denote positive growth. In short, people who make these choices learn. Choices to reject or deny new knowledge denote foreclosure, a stall in growth. In transformative learning terms, such a stall reflects an interrupted narrative.

Responses to encounter experiences will vary over the course of a person's lifetime and life conditions. Sometimes an individual will encounter, learn, and grow. Other times the force of the experience may be overwhelming and take more time to process. There is no pinnacle of racial identity development (Tatum, 1997), nor should there be for transformative learning. As learning is lifelong, people can and should recycle through the phases (Cross & Fhagen-Smith, 2001).

Teaching with Racial Identity Development Intentions

The bags that many students bring to campus are full of the national discourse of politically correct colorblindism. This discourse minimizes the awareness of race, while the everyday impacts of race persist (Essed, 1991; King, 1991). In this vein, colorblindism may be well intentioned, but upon critical reflection it is clear that this widely held habit of mind serves to preserve White racial dominance (Chávez & Guido-DiBrito, 1999; King, 1991). Dubbed *dysconsciousness* by Joyce E. King (1991), colorblindism is "an uncritical habit of mind (including perceptions, attitudes, assumptions, and beliefs) that justifies inequity and exploitation that accepts the given order of things as given. . . . [It] is a form of racism that tacitly accepts dominant White norms and privileges" (p. 135).

A more wholistic understanding of race and racism can be fostered when we teach with developmental intention (Taylor, 2000) regarding race. Through the creation of a disorienting dilemma or triggering event,[2] educators can provide an encounter experience, presenting students with the opportunity to cycle or recycle through racial identity processes. It is the role of the educator to present the racial challenge, providing the opportunity for students to transform their habits of mind (Mezirow, 2000) around the salience of race.

In consultation with scholars across three continents and reflection on their own practices, Taylor, Marienau, and Fiddler (2000) analyzed the literature of adult learning and development and found that educators believed that the process of arriving at developmental outcomes was most important. In particular, the researchers found that educators fostered student learning through experiential learning techniques, which according to Taylor (2000) meant that, "rather than depend on information *about* something, learners were encouraged to *experience* something" (p. 163). This emphasis on experiential learning is rooted in the theoretical frameworks of David Kolb (1984) and has been found to be pedagogically beneficial in a range of disciplines within higher education, as well as in more generally developing cultural awareness and democratic engagement (Nagada, Gurin, & Lopez, 2003). In particular Chávez and Guido-DiBrito (1999) contend that in making visible the invisible influence of race, the learning of all students is enhanced. For students of color, heightening the awareness of race creates a safe learning environment. White students benefit from exposure to the "multicultural skills, an enhanced ability to compare and contrast multiple perspectives, and keen reflective and observational abilities" that students of color develop out of necessity, given hostile and sometimes abusive learning environments (Chavez & Guido-DiBrito, 1999, p. 45; *see also* King, 1991).

Unpacking Excess Color-Blind Baggage: A Transformative Learning Point for Racial Identity Development

To illustrate how ideas of racial identity development and transformative learning theory can be bridged to understand better how students begin to transform habits of mind around race, we observed student reactions to an experiential exercise aimed at bringing awareness of White privilege. We held a combined class session of our graduate education courses, with a total of 27 students: 18 White, 8 African American, and 1 Native American. Of the 27 students, 20 were women—5 Black, 15 White. We submitted to students a survey developed by Peggy McIntosh (1988), which lists 50 everyday privileges associated with Whiteness. Students were to check each of the survey prompts containing a privilege that they perceived themselves as having. In the second stage of the exercise, students were to stand up while the faculty counted back from 50 the number of privileges. As a student's total number of privileges was called, he or she was to sit down. As expected, White students sat first and generally counted privileges in the range of 30–50, with White men generally sitting before women. Students of color generally saw themselves as having 15 privileges or less. Within these broader categorizations, younger and female students sat before older and male students. At the end of this stage, students wrote another reflection, and we began class discussion about the exercise.

In evaluating students' written reflections throughout the exercise, we found that graduate students' reactions to White privilege are strongly linked to racial identity development. Data were interpreted according to the "constant comparative" method (Strauss & Corbin, 1998). Although this exercise has limited generalizability because of sampling size and selection, geography, and other factors, this study provides an opportunity to analyze the intersection of student race and racial identity development and the effectiveness of using experiential learning to prompt students toward changing habits of mind around race. Given the composition of our sample, we decided to focus on the responses of women. The contrast in students' responses was most apparent when we compared the reactions in Black and White.

Black, White, and Raw

By the end of our classroom experiment, we found that most of the women were receptive to exploring the endemic nature of racism in society. This perspective on race, however, was not the one that most of the women brought in their knapsacks.

Women of both racial groups expressed dis-ease with the exercise. For example, a White woman in her mid-twenties admitted, "The term 'white privilege' makes me have uneasy feelings sitting in a room with African Americans." Similarly a Black woman in her early thirties asserted, "I live a comfortable life for the most part and feel 'normal' most of the time." For both women, the exercise served as an "outing" experience, challenging them to assess critically how they as individuals internalize matters of race. The accompanying discomfort, a pervasive theme throughout the study, is healthy, however—a direct response to the exercise as an encounter/triggering event and a first step toward changing habits of mind with regard to race.

White female graduate students in our study began largely in a pre-encounterlike existence (Cross & Fhagen-Smith, 2001; Hardiman, 2001), as if they had never confronted racial issues. Their bags were full of dysconscious color-blind ideological discourse. An engaging conversation on racial matters would have been impossible because these women did not have a sense of the ways in which race matters in contemporary life. In fact, these women seemed more interested in the manipulability of the survey instrument and in the number of the race prompts that could be exchanged for gender prompts to highlight male privilege. For example, a White woman aged 51 acknowledged racial privilege from the beginning, asserting, "The white privilege that I enjoy is something that I am usually not conscious of unless it is brought to my attention," but she asserted her "acute" awareness "of the limitations which are placed upon me due to my gender."

The White women participants, contrary to their conceptions of their racialized selves, had much vested in their gender identities. Without the exercise, time spent discussing racial matters probably would have been accompanied by parallel internal discussions that gender matters too. From a

transformative learning perspective, the exercise was a triggering event caus-
ing students to reflect on their racialized selves. For these women, a point of
connectedness, an experience, was needed to extend empathy beyond a sense
of lack of gender privilege (Belenky, Clinchy, Goldberger, & Tarule, 1986;
Flannery, 2000).

That connectivity, however, was not uniformly distributed. One of the
women, in her mid-twenties, began by expressing outright resistance and de-
fiance to the exercise: "This survey made me feel very uncomfortable because
it is obvious which answers you desire. . . . This survey appears to be very
biased and was not an appropriate learning tool." Even after the dramatic
display of White students sitting well before students of color, this woman
remained developmentally foreclosed, denying what she had just witnessed:
"Are people *really* treated in this manner? Perhaps I am naïve but it seems
farfetched to me that things of that actually go on." From her perspective,
no longer are there just two Black professors but, including students, a total
of 11 people of color conspiring to make her believe that "things of that go
on." She cannot even name the "it"—racism. Another student, in her late
twenties, suggested, "Maybe it's my white naiveté as I have been told before
by Professor——[Black] . . . that keeps me from seeing life 'outside of my
own world.'"

Note how these two women resist knowledge of race and racism, with
the latter directly challenging the competence of Black women faculty, not
to mention the White woman who designed this tried-and-true standard instrument. This type of reasoning is based in a subjective, guttural knowledge,
as articulated by Belenky et al. (1986). These women, and the latter woman
in particular, are developmentally foreclosed from grasping the ways in
which race matters (Hardiman, 2001; West, 2004).

Helms (1984) describes the naiveté and resistance that Whites express in
reaction to information about race and racism as indicators of the Contact
and Disintegration phases of her White Racial Identity Development
(WRID) model. Racial confrontation can be jarring for people in these
stages, and a withdrawal to color-blind norms provides safety and reassurance (Helms, 1984; Hardiman, 2001). Further self-imposed segregation may
follow so as to avoid future discomforting racial encounters. The Contact
and Disintegration phases are not psychologically healthy. In terms of transformative learning theory, a student in denial may stand "in grave danger of

growing" (Kegan, 1994, p. 293); however, this growth can be delayed or alto-
gether averted (Daloz, 1988; cf. Cohen & Piper, 2000). Given the context of
most predominantly White educational institutions, White students in these
phases can control intercultural interactions and the degree to which they
will move forward in their learning transformations and racial identity development. Aversion itself is a function of privilege (Helms, 1984).

While White women in the study were poised in pre-encounter states,
the fact of being Black did not correspond with states of racial identity development pinnacles for Black women in the study. Their bags were full too,
largely with pain regarding past racialized experiences. These women were
most interested in putting racial issues behind them in order to focus on
scholastic and labor-market goals. For some of the women, bringing up issues of racial privilege put them on the spot—it is an area of deficit for
women who otherwise seem to have their lives together.

One woman in particular felt that the exercise made the fact that she
was Black more obvious and highlighted the marginalization that quite often
comes with being Black, particularly in professional fields such as higher education administration. While acknowledging her Blackness, she expressed a
need to distance herself from negative imagery of African Americans. She
stated, "By the essence of my existence, I cope with racism and sexism in a
variety of realms. . . . On the other hand, my upbringing, lifestyle, education
and experience have allowed me to transcend many, although not all, of the
stereotypical challenges of minorities. I live a comfortable life for the most
part and feel 'normal' most of the time." As the survey was not about African
American stereotypes but White privilege, the reaction from this student
may be an indicator of internalized racism. She is distinguishing the "stereotypical challenges of minorities" and the comfort of her "normal" life, as if
race is not a challenge for her. "Normal" in this context is seemingly associated with a middle-class lifestyle that allows for purposeful color blindness,
inattention to matters of race, as most of those matters do not impinge on
her class-based comfort. In this manner, she and others poised as "excep-
tional Blacks" have class-based privileges that allow them to overlook matters
of race and gender while achieving "success."

Quite directly, this class-based sense of normalcy and transcendence indicates low race salience. According to Cross and Fhagen-Smith (2001), race
salience is a function of one's pattern of Nigrescence, one's path toward becoming "Black."[3]

The low race salience displayed by this student makes her a prime target for Nigrescence because, should they encounter a racial cultural incident, experience, or episode which exhausts the explanatory powers of their extant, nonrace-oriented frame of reference, they might go through Nigrescence as a means of radically changing their frame of reference. As long as low race salience persons are able to find an ecological niche that supports and sustains their identities, Nigrescence will not be triggered. . . . in the face of an Encounter which requires an explanatory system that does give salience to race and Black culture, such persons essentially have no answers. (p. 260)

The race salience of the other African American women in the study was higher. Rather than distancing themselves from the racialized nature of the experience, they expressed disillusionment due to the disjuncture of privileges that should be available on the account of class but are not. Taking a transcendental approach, one of the women said, "This reflective experience challenged me to take a look at a variety of circumstances to examine my comfort and confidence in who I am." She continued, "I had to constantly refocus to respond based on current states and not what I'd hope to view as privileges." While this woman finds her class privileges to be of comfort, she does not distance herself from less privileged African Americans. In this manner, she acknowledges that, class notwithstanding, race matters. Educational privileges can function similarly to and in conjunction with class-based privileges. Harking back to educational privilege, a Black woman in her mid-thirties simply stated, "Given my strong educational background, I still cannot walk through nor enjoy the same privileges as my white counterparts." In an educational setting, such a recognition can mean a baseline acceptance of a student's ability and qualifications to be successful in the campus classroom (Chávez & Guido-DiBrito, 1999).

The women in our study employed a number of coping mechanisms to deal with the harsh reality that the survey triggered them to recall. For example, a Black woman in her early twenties found humor as an outlet. She stated, "This exercise makes me laugh because I was asked to circle each statement that applied to me. Each statement was about white privilege, and since I am not white I circled 10 of 50. No surprise there." Humor may be employed here as a coping mechanism, allowing lightness to facilitate the assimilation of grave and hurtful information. A Black woman in her late twenties expressed sadness in connection with the exercise, reflecting on "how much race influences American society." Her defensive strategy is to insulate herself from American racism by working "in an environment where my race is welcome. Where black employees can speak up and be heard without penalty." She works at a historically Black university.

It appears that most of the Black women students, rather than being in a pre-encounter state, are arriving at or recycling to the immersion-emersion phase (Cross, 1973). They have found ways to cope with, and integrate, their personal knowledge of race and racism. The exercise, however, seems to have stirred up latent pain and perhaps anger and frustration.

Recycling in one's racial identity development raises the question of whether recycling occurs in transformative learning processes. Extending Edward Cell's (1984) notion that there are learning benefits to revisiting one's past experiences, we posit that rather than a linear process, transformative education has cyclical elements akin to a spiral staircase. As we progress, we do so in parallel rounds.[4] Cell's work suggests that new learning is generated when old experiences are analyzed from a new perspective, given present positions on the staircase (1984). Taking Cell's thoughts a step further, a person can engage in parallel experiences, creating new narratives and opportunities for further growth around old issues. In this vein, the Black women in our study were able to reflect anew on race and racism. At best, this experience helped them recycle through Nigrescence and toward a more integrated understanding of their racial identity development (Cross & Fhagen-Smith, 2001). At worst, they were able to reflect on the color line (Du Bois, 2004), extending the struggle for racial understanding even into this new millennium.

Steps Toward Transformation and Learning

Despite one student's resistance, all the women in our study were able to draw on the experience and connect with care and concern for the future. Although the works of Belenky et al. (1986) and Hayes and Flannery (2000) generally restrict the power of connection to White women, Patricia Hill Collins's (2000) work in the area of Black feminism highlights the importance of connectivity in the assimilation and integration of knowledge for Black women. Most dramatically, in this exercise, one Black woman with male children, after seeing two Black men as the last students standing, totally disregarded her own personal racialized experience, detailed in her first reflection, and focused on the plight of her children. A White woman in her mid-thirties whose husband is African American/Black expressed similar concern for their future children: "It [the survey] also brings fears to my mind about how my children will fare."

Yet the point of connectivity for the majority of the women was toward the general state of the world: Will it ever change? It is at this point, after the disorienting dilemma/triggering encounter, that students took their first steps toward transforming their habits of mind around race. Said a White woman in her mid-twenties, "What we do with the privilege we have is the key. Do we use it for good or bad?" With a newly found racial awareness, this woman is poised to integrate this tangible knowledge and further develop her racial identity. This woman has, in fact, learned something. Her future individual and collective action will display whether transformative learning or mere critical reflection actually occurred (Brookfield, 2000).

We believe that the learning inspired by the exercise is deep, as reflected in the realist approach of the participants with regard to future struggles for racial equality. Expressing guilt and frustration, a White woman in her early thirties asked, "How, as white people, do we instigate change?" Defining the issue of privilege as a zero-sum game, she questioned, "Are we willing to help change, because it [change] will assure the loss of privilege we've held onto for so long." A White woman aged twenty-five also acknowledged the intergenerational nature of privilege: "These privileges are handed or passed down from generation to generation. We inherit these privileges mostly because of our race." Her words echo an emerging literature that highlights ways in which the intergenerational transmission of wealth carries forward the persistence of gaps in the attainment of status between Blacks and Whites (Conley, 1999; Shapiro, 2004).

The responses of the women in the study also reflect a road toward transformation that begins with little steps as opposed to instant, Damascus-like change. These women are contemplating how much they have to give up in order to obtain the worthy goal of transformation, a goal that benefits distant others at their individual expense. It is in this respect that discourse on diversity is most poignant. When we consider a fixed set of resources, such as seat allocation in college admissions, the pie is limited, and the only way to achieve equity is to redistribute. However, thinking globally about diversity as growing the pie by making people more connected, learned, empathetic, and civically engaged, in addition to being more profitable in business

(Milem, 2003), the dialogue shifts from a zero-sum short term to win-win in the long run.

One Black woman in her thirties shared the pain that was conjured by the exercise and by her reflections on the cyclical failings of Americans to achieve racial harmony, but in spite of that pain, she has recycled. She stated, "I hold hope in my heart (in spite of my frustrations) that one day we will achieve civil and human rights in their purest, most sacred forms in all things." This woman expresses what Cornell West describes as "tragic hope" (2004). In terms of racial identity development, the point at which she has arrived is emersion, a merger of racial knowledge with an inner peace regarding its existence (Cross & Fhagen-Smith, 2001). Emersion is the healthiest phase of racial identity development. Although this woman's journey was not without hazard, she too appears to have survived the danger and grown (Kegan, 1994).

Implications for Practice

Although the generalizability of the findings of this exercise are limited, we do learn that through unpacking excess racial baggage, learners can grow multicultural awareness and transform their habits of mind around race and racism. In presenting the disorienting dilemma/triggering event encounters, however, educators should appreciate the pedagogical implications of the differences that students bring to learning enterprises. With this caveat in mind, we suggest three recommendations for practice:

1. Specific goal-directed transformative learning aimed at racial and gender awareness: blending experiential and scholarly learning opportunities when addressing matters of social controversy. On the whole, our presentation of an exercise on White privilege before entering into a deeper discussion of race was instructive. We wanted our discussion to be meaningful, and given the level of introspection in which most of the women engaged, this much we achieved. It is likely that many of these women, without opportunity to see and develop empathy, would have largely remained foreclosed to the idea that race still matters, while others preferred to forget. Taylor (2000) emphasizes the importance of the experience in experiential learning, but graduate students especially need the content, the theoretical bases to understand their individual experience, as well as to contribute effectively to the broader scholarly knowledge base. Moreover, discussions and experiences with issues of race and racism in our classes were not one-time events. We revisited the concepts and ideas throughout the remainder of the course, encouraging students to make connections between course content and the experiential exercise.

2. *Respecting diversity of experiences and ideas within groups.* Discourse requires awareness and inclusion of diverse perspectives within and across racial and gender lines. How we engage around these topics, however, is not without challenge because of the loaded nature of individuals' bags. The responses of the women in our study reflected overlapping identities of race, class, gender, sexual orientation, religion, marital status, and so on. Although there was much convergence along racial lines with respect to connectivity, empathy, and pain, at the outset there was a diversity of opinion as to whether and how race matters. Color blindness is a dominant theme in popular conceptions of race, with significant prevalence in academia (King, 1991). Therefore, assuming that we carry similar bags along racial lines is fallacious stereotyping. The implication is that educators should avoid positioning particular students as tokens, one-person representatives of some group. The pain that the Black women in our study, in particular, demonstrated reveals that they would rather not be put on the spot. Although we as good educators want to further in-class dialogue on many controversial matters, singling out students may have the effect of evoking such pain in an unbalanced manner. In our exercise, everyone shared their personal experiences, which had group implications, but ultimately students spoke on behalf of their individual selves.

3. *Collaboration between student and academic affairs around matters of race and culture.* The context of the multicultural campus provides a unique environment for people to explore various cultures while developing their own racial identity. Deliberate learning goals can be set, achieved, and reinforced when student affairs and the academic arenas work deliberately toward integrating book knowledge about race with tangible experiences. Toward that end, campuses should encourage events that highlight a multiplicity of cultures and cosponsor multicultural events across lines of race, gender, sexual orientation, religion, and so on. In this vein, students attending events in support of their particular organizational affiliation can engage with students in other organizations, students with whom they otherwise may not socialize. Through deliberately planned academic and social engagement, we can create conditions whereby students are encouraged to examine and reexamine their bags.

Notes

1. During the early post–Civil Rights era, psychologists became aware of the limited applicability of the Erikson (1963) model of identity development as applied to African Americans. Toward this end, models of racial identity development were constructed, beginning with models of Black identity (Cross, 1973; Cross & Fhagen-Smith, 2001), and emerged to include White identity development (Hardiman, 1979, 2001; Helms, 1984), ethnic identity development (Chávez & Guido-DiBrito, 1999; Ferdaman & Gallegos, 2001; Kim, 2001) and multiracial/ethnic identity development (Root, 1996; Wijeyesinghe, 2001).

2. In transformative learning theory, the difference between disorienting dilemmas and triggering events marks the degree of "trauma," with the former likened to St. Paul's Damascus Road experience and the latter as a starting point for a series of events culminating in transformation.

3. For a more detailed discussion of Cross's Nigrescence theory and patterns of African American identity development, see Cross & Fhagen-Smith (2001).

4. Note here that the imagery of a staircase dictates that just as steps can be taken forward, steps can also be taken backward. Full analysis of the staircase metaphor, along with the concept of backward steps, is beyond the scope of this chapter.

References

Badu, E. (2000). Bag lady. On *Mama's gun* [CD]. New York: Motown Records.

Belenky, M. F., Clinchy, B. M., Goldberger, N. R., & Tarule, J. M. (1986). *Women's ways of knowing: The development of self, voice, and mind.* New York: Basic Books.

Bennett, J. M., & Bennett, M. J. (2004). Developing intercultural sensitivity: An integrative approach to global and domestic diversity. In D. Landis, J. M. Bennett, & M. J. Bennett (Eds.), *Handbook of intercultural training* (3rd ed., pp. 147–165). Thousand Oaks, CA: Sage.

Blackmun, J. (1978). University of California Board of Regents v. Bakke, 438 U.S. 265, 407.

Brookfield, S. D. (2000). The concept of critically reflective practice. In A. Wilson & E. Hayes (Eds.), *Handbook 2000 of adult and continuing education* (pp. 33–50). San Francisco: Jossey-Bass.

Cell, Edward. (1984). *Learning to learn from experience.* Albany: State University of New York Press.

Chávez, A. F., & Guido-DiBrito, F. (1999). Racial and ethnic identity and development. *New Directions for Adult and Continuing Education, 84,* 39–47.

Cohen, A. (1998). *The shaping of American higher education: Emergence and growth of the contemporary system.* San Francisco: Jossey-Bass.

Cohen, J. B., & Piper, D. (2000). Transformation in a residential adult learning community. In J. Mezirow & Associates (Eds.), *Learning as transformation: Critical perspectives on a theory in progress*. San Francisco: Jossey-Bass.

Collins, P. H. (2000). *Black feminist thought: Knowledge, consciousness, and the politics of empowerment* (2nd ed.). New York: Routledge Press.

Conley, D. (1999). *Being black, living in the red: Race, wealth, and social policy in America*. Berkeley: University of California Press.

Cross, W. E., Jr. (1973). The Negro-to-Black conversion experience. In J. A. Ladner (Ed.), *The death of White sociology* (pp. 267–286). New York: Vintage Books.

Cross, W. E., Jr., & Fhagen-Smith, P. (2001). Patterns of African American identity development: A life span perspective. In C. L. Wijeyesinghe & B. W. Jackson (Eds.), *New perspectives on racial identity development: A theoretical and practical anthology* (pp. 242–270). New York: New York University Press.

Daloz, L. A. (1988). The story of Gladys who refused to grow: A morality tale for mentors. *Lifelong Learning, 11*(4), 4–7.

Du Bois, W. E. B. (2004). *The souls of Black folk, 100th Anniversary Edition*. Boulder, CO: Paradigm.

Erikson, E. H. (1963). *Childhood and society* (2nd ed.). New York: Norton.

Essed, P. (1991). *Understanding everyday racism: An interdisciplinary theory*. Newbury Park, CA: Sage.

Ferdman, B.M. & Gallegos, P. I. (2001). Latinos and racial identity development. In C. L. Wijeyesinghe & B. W. Jackson III (Eds.), New perspectives on racial identity development: A theoretical and practical anthology (pp. 32–66). New York: New York University Press.

Flannery, D. D. (2000). Connection. In E. Hayes & D. D. Flannery (Eds.), *Women as learners: The significance of gender in adult learning* (pp. 111–137). San Francisco: Jossey-Bass.

Hardiman, R. (1979). *White identity development: A process oriented model for describing the racial consciousness of White Americans*. Unpublished doctoral dissertation, University of Massachusetts, Amherst.

Hardiman, R. (2001). Reflections on white identity development theory. In C. L. Wijeyesinghe & B. W. Jackson (Eds.), *New perspectives on racial identity development: A theoretical and practical anthology* (pp. 109–128). New York: New York University Press.

Hayes, E., & Flannery, D. D. (Eds.) (2000). *Women as learners: The significance of gender in adult learning*. San Francisco: Jossey-Bass.

Helms, J. E. (1984). Towards a theoretical explanation of the effects of race on counseling: A Black and White model. *Counseling Psychologist, 12*(4), 153–165.

hooks, b. (1995). Black women: Shaping feminist theory. In B. Guy-Sheftall (Ed.), *Words of fire: An anthology of African-American feminist thought* (pp. 270–282). New York: New Press. (Essay originally published 1981)

Johnson, J. L. (2001). *Harlemworld: Doing race and class in contemporary Black America*, Chicago: University of Chicago Press.

Kegan, R. (1994). *In over our heads: The mental demands of modern life*. Cambridge, MA: Harvard University Press.

Kim, J. (2001). Asian American identity development theory. In C. L. Wijeyesinghe, & Jackson III, B.W. (Eds.), *New perspectives on racial identity development: A theoretical and practical anthology* (pp. 67–90). New York: New York University Press.

King, J. E. (1991). Dysconscious racism: Ideology, identity, and the miseducation of teachers. *Journal of Negro Education, 60*(2), 133–146.

Kolb, D. A. (1984). *Experiential learning: Experience as a source of learning and development*. Englewood Cliffs, NJ: Prentice Hall.

McIntosh, P. (1988). *White privilege and male privilege: A personal account of coming to see correspondences through work in women's studies* (Working Paper 189). Wellesley, MA: Wellesley College Center for Research on Women.

Mezirow, J. (2000). Learning to think like an adult: Core concepts of transformation theory. In J. Mezirow & Associates (Eds.), *Learning as transformation: Critical perspectives on a theory in progress*. San Francisco: Jossey-Bass.

Milem, J. F. (2003). The educational benefits of diversity: Evidence from multiple sectors. In M. J. Chang et al. (Eds.), *Compelling interest: Examining the evidence on racial dynamics in higher education* (pp. 126–168). Stanford, CA: Stanford University Press.

Nagada, B. R. A., Gurin, P., & Lopez, G. E. (2003). Transformative pedagogy for democracy and social justice. *Race Ethnicity and Education, 6*(2), 165–191.

Rankin, S. R., & Reason, R. D. (2005). Differing perceptions: How students of color and White students perceive campus climate for underrepresented groups. *Journal of College Student Development, 46*(1), 43–61.

Root, M. P. (Ed.) (1996) *The multiracial experience: Racial borders as the new frontier*. Thousand Oaks, CA: Sage Publications.

Shapiro, T. M. (2004). *The hidden costs of being African American: How wealth perpetuates inequality*. Oxford, UK: Oxford University Press.

Sheared, V. (1994). Giving voice: An inclusive model of instruction—A womanist perspective. *New Directions for Adult and Continuing Education, 61*, 27–37.

Strauss, A. L. & Corbin, J. M. (1998). *Basics of qualitative research: Techniques and procedures for developing grounded theory*. Thousand Oaks, CA: Sage.

Swim J. K., Hyers, L. L., Cohen, L. L., & Ferguson, M. J. (2001). Everyday sexism: Evidence for its incidence, nature, and psychological impact from three daily diary studies. *Journal of Social Issues, 57*(1), 31–53.

Tatum, B. D. (1997). *"Why are all the Black kids sitting together in the cafeteria?" A psychologist explains the development of racial identity*. New York: Basic Books.

Taylor, K. (2000). Teaching with developmental intention. In J. Mezirow & Associates (Eds.), *Learning as transformation: Critical perspectives on a theory in progress.* San Francisco: Jossey-Bass.

Taylor, K., Marienau, C., & Fiddler, M. (2000). *Developing adult learners: Strategies for teachers and trainers.* San Francisco: Jossey-Bass.

U.S. Department of Education. (2004). Total fall enrollment in degree-granting institutions, by race/ethnicity, sex, attendance status, and level of student: Selected years, 1976 to 2002. Washington, DC: U.S. Department of Education, National Center for Education Statistics. Retrieved May 9, 2006, from http://nces.ed.gov/programs/digest/d04/tables/dt04_206.asp

Watson, L. W., Terrell, M. C., Wright, D. J., & Associates. (2002). *How minority students experience college: Implications for planning and policy.* Sterling, VA: Stylus.

West, C. (2004). *Democracy matters: Winning the fight against imperialism.* New York: Penguin.

Wijeyesinghe, C. L. (2001). Racial identity in multiracial people: An alternative paradigm. In C. L. Wijeyesinghe & B. W. Jackson III (Eds.), *New perspectives on racial identity development: A theoretical and practical anthology* (pp. 129–152). New York: University.

Wijeyesinghe, C. L., & Jackson, B. W. III. (Eds.) (2001). *New perspectives on racial identity development: A theoretical and practical anthology.* New York: New York University Press.

7

IS MONA LISA STILL SMILING?

Women and the Out-of-Class Experience

Jeanie K. Allen

For the past two years in my Introduction to Women's Studies class, we have viewed *Mona Lisa Smile* (Newell, Goldsmith-Thomas, Schlindler, & Schiff, 2004), a film advertised, strangely, as a romantic comedy. For those who have not seen the film, it depicts the lives of college women in 1953 at (fictional) Wellesley College, where a new art history professor, played by Julia Roberts, begins teaching in ways that she hopes will transform the young female students so that they view their lives as their own, encouraging them to create their own path rather than follow the societal expectations of marrying, having children, and devoting their lives solely to their families. After the class views the film, I ask my students, "Is this still the way it is in college?" At first they respond with giggles, citing how different the clothing, hairstyles, and rules are from today. As we deconstruct this film, however, noticing the overwhelming pressure for these young women to marry, the prevalence of discussions surrounding romance rather than academic issues, the double standard applied to men's and women's sexuality, and the compromises that the young women are willing to make in order to be married, while always displaying the smile that tells the world how happy they are, a silence fills the room. Soon, my students begin citing examples of ways in which the culture on campus remains similar to this film about college women in the 1950s.

The peer culture on many college campuses promotes the idea that, for women, heterosexual romantic relationships should take priority over academics (Holland & Eisenhart, 1990). When women students begin college, they tend to discuss doing well academically; soon after arriving on campus, however, many of their conversations tend to center on their relationships with men. Women's status is often judged by their attractiveness, defined as the status of the men whom they seem to attract. Although male students are also judged by the women whom they seem to attract, men, more often than women, also receive recognition for their achievements in and out of the classroom and for their leadership positions. This tendency for female learners to place academics as subordinate to romantic relationships promotes a *sorority* orientation to sisterhood, defined as women seeing other women as rivals for the attention of men, defining themselves in terms of their relationships with men, and accepting the role of dependency on men (Gmelch, 1998). This peer culture is actually far more influential than academics on the student experience, with many students sensing their course work to be completely separate from *their lives.*

Although these findings may prove disheartening to some people, during the 15 years since Holland and Eisenhart (1990) published their study on the peer culture's emphasis on romance, progress has been made. Women are now entering professional programs and graduate schools in ever growing numbers. But the out-of-classroom experience for undergraduate students continues to present some daunting problems.

In a recent report, the American Association of University Women (AAUW) Educational Foundation states that 66% of all undergraduate students experience some type of sexual harassment during their college years, but few students report these behaviors to an authority (Hill & Silva, 2005). Male students note that they are often harassed by other men and by women, usually being the victims of verbal assaults using derogatory, homophobic terms. Women students, however, indicate that they are harassed more often by male students, both verbally and physically. The AAUW report states that 50% of the male students admitted that they had harassed another student, with 25% indicating that they harassed others often or occasionally; approximately one third of the female students acknowledged participating in sexual harassment, usually aimed at men (Hill & Silva, 2005). Reactions to sexual harassment differ for men and women. Male students report that they are most often annoyed by this behavior. Female students, on the other hand, note that they feel angry, confused, and less confident in their abilities to succeed in college. In addition, these women often find themselves attempting to avoid the harassers, even going as far as failing to attend class or take part in out-of-class activities. Sadly, students state that harassment is just part of college and that they are just having fun (Hill & Silva, 2005).

In addition to the problem of sexual harassment, and considered related to it, is the prevalence of binge drinking on campuses (Elkins, Helms, & Pierson, 2003). Citing this as one of, if not the, most prevalent out-of-class problem for students in college, researchers have found that students report that they drink in order to get drunk, with many men and women reporting drinking at least five or four drinks, respectively, in one setting. Not discounting the health effects of excessive alcohol consumption, a significant correlation between drinking alcohol and sexual aggression posits another problem in the out-of-class experience (Kaly, Heesacker, & Frost, 2002). Research indicates that acquaintance rape and risky sexual behaviors occur far more often when alcohol is involved. Additionally, research has found that men are more likely to misinterpret signals when female students have been drinking, often resulting in unwanted sexual overtures and even sexual violence. Unfortunately, when women have been consuming alcohol, the blame for sexual misconduct tends to fall on them. Once again, the prevalence of the peer culture places all students at risk, posing even more serious consequences for women.

The prevalence of pressure on women students to pursue heterosexual romantic relationships, to go along with and participate in sexual harassment for fun, and to engage in excessive alcohol consumption paints a picture of an out-of-class experience that undermines their success. Although these kind of behaviors are explicit, Hall and Sandler (1984) contend that many covert signals promote what they call a "chilly climate." Do we still see women students being asked to serve in traditional gender roles during campus activities, such as preparing and serving food or cleaning up? How often do people wear or display T-shirts and posters that demean women or portray them as sexual objects, all in the name of fun? Are events related to so-called women's issues still underattended or ridiculed? Most campuses continue to create rules and regulations to address some of these issues, but an examination of the ways students make meaning out of the peer culture illuminates potential strategies for assisting all students with the out-of-class experience.

Making Meaning

When examining the out-of-class experience, the meaning that students make of their experiences is relevant, but in order to address some of the environmental factors, the more important question is *how* they make sense of campus life. In this chapter the out-of class experience is examined through the lenses of two constructive-developmental theories, those of Kegan (1982) and Baxter Magolda (1992). Kegan provides a model of development, proposing evolving orders of consciousness, such that individuals develop the potential to advance those tendencies in which they are embedded (subject) to elements on which they can reflect (object). Each of these orders of consciousness subsumes the previous one, but it is the evolution and transitions that are the focus, not the arrival at some static stage, that Kegan encourages educators to consider.

Young children shift from a stage at which they are subject to their impulses to one at which they can reflect on those impulses yet become subject to their needs, interests, and wishes (Kegan, 1982). Kegan names this first position the *impulsive* stage and the second stage the *imperial.* In the time from middle childhood to early adulthood, individuals evolve from being subject to their needs to reflecting on those needs, becoming subject to the desire for interpersonal relationships or, in Kegan's terms, moving from the imperial to the *interpersonal*, stage 3. With additional development, individuals then progress from the interpersonal to the *institutional*, stage 4, or in other words, to reflecting on relationships yet becoming subject to the process of authoring identities and ideologies. In stage 5 of this model, which is noted as an extremely rare position, Kegan proposes that people evolve from the institutional to the *interindividual*, reflecting on the process of authoring their lives while becoming subject to viewing themselves as part of an interdependent system. Kegan notes that fewer than one third to one half of all adults ever reach the fourth order, institutional, yet in a later work, Kegan (1994) suggests that modern life requires adults to operate from this perspective.

For most traditional-aged college students, the process of development involves the transition from Kegan's (1982) interpersonal stage to the institutional, or what has been termed "The Great Accommodation" (Love & Guthrie, 1999). As students enter college, they experience a sort of culture shock, encountering new and sometimes hidden values, behaviors, and even language. For most of these students, they are embedded in their desire to belong, seeking relationships with other students. If the culture demands certain behaviors that contribute to a sexist, and often homophobic, environment, many students are faced with choosing to go along or be alienated from the group. If, in fact, most of these students are, at best, in the transition from third- to fourth-order thinking in Kegan's model, then the choice to go against these norms creates a sense of loss and alienation rather than a source of empowerment and conscious action based on a carefully self-constructed set of values. Kegan (1994) asks educators whether the campus environment assumes that students are capable of fourth-order thinking when faced with these fourth-stage dilemmas.

Kegan (1994) does not directly cite gender differences in his theoretical model but rather indicates that the evolution of orders of consciousness centers around a lifelong tension between autonomy and connection. He notes that women's tendency to place a higher value on connection does not describe a lesser position of development, reminding the reader that though he describes a model progressing toward self-authorship, deciding for oneself does not mean deciding by oneself (Kegan, 1994). In fact, he argues that in his model, the highest order does not reflect a move toward independence and separateness but rather an identity that also integrates connection and relationships.

Marcia Baxter Magolda (1992) presents another model of development toward more complex ways of knowing, labeling this, perhaps, same tension between autonomy and connection as gender related. She describes two different paths through the developmental stages, one followed by more women than men and the other preferred by more men than women. The broad stages of this model appear similar to other models (Belenky, Clinchy, Goldberger, & Tarule, 1986; Perry, 1970) in which students seem to progress from *absolute* knowing—in which knowledge is certain, the professor is the authority, and peers can share material and explain some concepts to one another—to *transitional* knowing, in which knowledge is certain in some disciplines and uncertain in others, the professor is the authority in the process of understanding the material, and peers can provide dialogue. From transitional knowing, students may shift to *independent* knowing, in which all knowledge is understood to be uncertain, but they accept this uncertainty because everyone has his or her own beliefs, the professor serves to promote sharing of student opinions, and peers begin to serve as sources of knowledge when and if they share their views. As students are asked to evaluate differing views on the basis of evidence, they can then move into *contextual* knowing, understanding that knowledge is always contextual, that the professor serves as a partner in the process of learning, and that peers are capable of providing new knowledge. The gender-related differences that were found in the first three stages merge in contextual knowing, when learners begin to integrate knowledge, evidence, and context. Baxter Magolda found that very few traditional-aged undergraduates reached contextual knowing by the time of graduation, and most appeared to remain in the evolution from transitional to independent patterns of knowing.

Through the first three ways of knowing, Baxter Magolda (1992) terms the gender-related path that more women than men follow a *relational* path and names the pattern used by more men than women an *abstract* path. Those learners following the relational path use a *receiving* pattern in the first stage, absolute knowing. These students seek a relaxed atmosphere, use listening as their primary way of learning, and resolve differences in opinions through personal interpretation. Those using the receiving pattern often do not speak in class, and their quiet demeanor is often misinterpreted as disinterest by the professor. When these relational learners progress to transitional knowing, their approach, labeled the *interpersonal,* becomes one of gathering material and ideas from others, wanting to hear others' views, and actually welcoming uncertainty. At this point, these students want to find their own voices and turn to their peers and friends to assist them with this process. As the relational learners enter independent knowing, their path is labeled the *interindividual.* They tend to become less concerned about what others think of them but still actively and openly seek an exchange of ideas with their peers. They continue to use listening as a pattern of gathering new knowledge but also want to understand through dialogue. Hearing others' interpretations and experiences helps them to clarify their own opinions. These students want a connection between their academics and their personal lives.

The students taking the abstract path use a *mastery* approach to learning in the absolute stage (Baxter Magolda, 1992). These learners enjoy debate and want the professors to know that they are participating and interested, almost seeking to imitate the professors. Students using a mastery approach actually have more difficulty evolving to transitional knowing than relational-oriented learners do. The abstract learners feel uncomfortable with uncertainty. They approach transitional knowing using an *impersonal* pattern; they still want to debate their peers, but they want to use research and outside evidence, rather than student interpretations, as the basis for understanding, thus shying away from using relationships for mastering the process of learning. For these students, the move toward independent knowing proves difficult because they maintain an external vision of certainty rather than see others and themselves as the constructers of knowledge. These abstract learners enter this next stage using an *individual* pattern of knowing. They have to work to listen to others but do listen because they hope to be able to change the other students' opinions. Thus, these students struggle to move toward relationships with others, finding difficulty with the idea of the equality of differing views.

Baxter Magolda (1992) notes that many first-year students are absolute knowers but that most students progress to transitional knowers by their junior year. Fewer than 5% of the students she interviewed reflected independent knowing at the time of graduation. Kegan (1982) indicates that while some first-year students enter in the imperial stage, most are involved in the transition from the interpersonal to the institutional. Integrating these two constructive-developmental theories could help educators to understand more fully how students are making meaning from the co-curriculum.

Integrating Models

Merging the models presented by these two theorists suggests that the majority of traditional undergraduates are transitional learners (Baxter Magolda) evolving from the interpersonal to the institutional orders of consciousness (Kegan). The overlapping terminology can be rather confusing; both authors use the term *interpersonal*, but with different meanings. For the sake of clarity, I will continue to use Baxter Magolda's (1992) terms *relational* (the path followed more often by women than men) and *abstract* (the path followed more often by men than women).Examining students through the lens of third-order thinking, Kegan (1994) suggests that these learners are capable of joining a community and speaking the "language" of the community but cannot reflect on being a member of that community. In this stage, young men and women respond to socialization but do not fully acknowledge that they can be responsible for the socialization process. The influences and expectations of others create the self, for these young people are not yet able to realize that they can create their own self and their own self-expectations. These students are afraid of losing relationships and will conform to the norms that appear to maintain their belongingness. Those students following the relational path suggest that they want to resolve uncertainty for themselves but prefer to use their peers for support. They seek to collect different perspectives from their friends but do not challenge those ideas. When faced with sexist or homophobic behavior, or pressure to consume excessive amounts of alcohol, the relational students will turn to their friends for support, but their peers most likely reinforce conformist behavior because of their own needs for belonging.

Those students following the abstract path also exhibit a strong need for belonging and are subject to their relationships. These learners, however, like to be challenged by their peers and debate ideas. They seek external sources of authority in order to resolve uncertainty. But the overriding factor in determining their final decisions regarding whether to go along with specific behaviors most likely is the need to remain a member of the community. Thus, they may debate whether some actions are "good," but to completely refuse to follow the crowd creates the risk of alienation. For both the relational and abstract students, if educators provide no source of intervention or assistance, these learners are left stranded with little support. When faculty and administrators then react to what is deemed offensive and irresponsible behavior, rather than expect these young men and women to navigate their own journey, Kegan (1994) and Baxter Magolda (1992) suggest that bridges be built to help students in their transitions to more complex ways of knowing.

Bridge Building

What does a bridge do? It provides a structure for individuals to move from one side to the other at their own pace, while feeling secure that the structure will hold them as they cross. Unlike the characters on *Star Trek,* however, these travelers are not beamed up to the other side. They have a starting place and must take their own steps. Kegan (1994) and Baxter Magolda and King (2004) remind educators that in order to help students through the transition to more complex ways of knowing, the bridge must start where students are, which encompasses what they know and how they know.

In order to construct this bridge, educators must reflect on the "other side." Where should this bridge go? Using the integrated model presented in the preceding section, a reasonable goal could be the transformation from the interpersonal to the institutional order of consciousness (Kegan, 1982). Students approaching fourth-order consciousness develop the capacity to *have* relationships rather than be *in* relationships. These fourth-order thinkers understand that they can construct their own values, that they are capable of working to help create the culture, and that they can set boundaries for themselves within relationships and organizations. Although Kegan (1994) refers to this dynamic as developing autonomy, he argues that autonomy means self-reliance and can be grounded in furthering relationships, which would not exclude the need for connection that is often referred to when discussing women's development.

In addition, this transformation includes the move to independent knowing (Baxter Magolda, 1992). Relational independent knowers use an interindividual style, in which they go beyond gathering other perspectives to voicing their views. They accept the uncertainty of knowledge and want peers to enter into discussions so that all sides are heard. These learners want peers and professors to act as partners in learning. Abstract independent knowers use an individual pattern. These students also want to share differing views, but they seek to maintain their own beliefs and values as the center of their focus. These abstract independent students desire to set their own goals, while also working toward considering others' perspectives as valid.

Using the bridge metaphor, each step across the way assists students in moving closer to the fourth-order/independent abilities. For the creators of these bridges, an important facet is the fact that many, if not most, students will not reach the other side before graduation. Thus, presenting the goal as completing the journey to the other side will probably overwhelm and possibly defeat students and frustrate educators. However, higher education does a great disservice to our students if these learners are asked to function from the other side of the bridge when they graduate, even though they have never seen how to begin to cross over or what might lie on the other side. One well-researched model that holds promise is the Learning Partnerships Model (Baxter Magolda & King, 2004).

The Learning Partnerships Model

The Learning Partnerships Model (LPM) resulted from a 17-year longitudinal study of college students as they passed through their university experience and beyond (Baxter Magolda & King, 2004). The creators of this approach began with the premise that a, if not the, major goal in higher education needs to be to assist students with their development toward contextual knowing and fourth-order thinking, referred to as *self-authorship* (Kegan, 1994). As Baxter Magolda, in this volume (p. 30), tells us, this goal provides a supportive environment for all learners, leading classroom educators to promote more active learning in the classroom and to give learners more opportunities to construct their own knowledge. Can this model help students navigate the out-of-class experience in ways that might alter the student culture to promote less sexist, homophobic, and destructive behaviors?

The LPM supports the idea of building a bridge by providing appropriate levels of challenge and support, giving individuals the desire and confidence necessary to cross the bridge. In order to entice students to begin the journey, educators need to challenge students to accept three assumptions: that knowledge is socially constructed and there will always be multiple perspectives to consider, that knowledge alters the self and one's identity, and that sharing perspectives and knowledge with others is imperative to further understanding (Baxter Magolda & King, 2004). Providing students with exercises that embody these three assumptions can prove threatening. Many undergraduates are embedded in relationships, struggling to balance autonomy and connection, and encountering confusion regarding the sources of authority. Thus, as important as challenging students to accept the three assumptions are three principles that reflect support for these learners: that their perspectives and judgments are welcome and respected, that their own knowledge and experience is relevant and important, and that all participants can be equal partners in constructing meaning. These principles of support provide students with a sense of security when the bridge seems to be swaying in the wind.

Can the LPM be implemented to help students navigate when they face a culture that appears to support sexist, homophobic, and destructive behaviors? Important to this question is evidence regarding what students feel is most important in their out-of-class lives. As part of a larger study investigating women's career choices during college, my colleague Kathleen Taylor and I interviewed 20 female seniors and asked them questions about their in-class and out-of-class experiences during college (Allen & Taylor, 2006). Although the initial purpose of this research was to study the differences between learners who appeared to have made a commitment for the time period following graduation and those students whose plans remained open, the comments from these young women provide insight into their campus lives. The following section presents themes that emerged from an inductive analysis of this qualitative study as these young women described their out-of-class experiences.

Themes from Student Interviews

The 20 participants in our study were traditional-aged female seniors within one year of graduation at the time of their interviews. These students attended a private liberal arts college in the Midwest, with a student population of approximately 1,500 students. All the interviewees were Caucasian, with 97% of the student body also being White. The interviews were conducted using an open-ended, guided interview approach. These students were selected as representative of women seniors who had explored a variety of majors, with 10 of the interviewees having committed to a postgraduation plan and 10 remaining in the search mode. The criteria for selection came from Josselson's (1996) work on identity and career decision-making. For more information on selection criteria and on Josselson's analysis, see the article that I published with Kathleen Taylor in the *Journal of College Student Development* (2006). The themes that emerged when examining these students' discussion of life outside the classroom were (a) romantic relationships, (b) family members, (c) the role of friends, (d) the real world versus school, and (e) what and where they learned.

Romantic Relationships

With regard to romantic relationships, 9 out of the 20 women interviewed declared that they would be marrying their current boyfriend and that this goal took priority in their planning process. Three of these students described their romantic relationship as "independent, but dependent at the same time" and described decision making as "mutual." It was obvious that these three couples had engaged in serious discussions about what each person wanted and how they could create a plan that allowed both of them to achieve their goals.

Six of these nine women were arranging their future plans in order to maintain their relationships with their boyfriends, waiting for their boyfriends to make decisions first and then planning to follow them. When

asked about their own personal desires, they tended to defer to their boyfriends' choices. When Debbie discussed her future plans, she told me,

> I'm trying to figure out how to maybe not have an artistic job, but a cre-
> ative job, but . . . I don't know . . . because I'm going to move to Boston
> . . . to be with Tom. I met him in London last semester. . . . we're pretty
> much perfect for each other. The only thing is, he's a junior and I'm a
> senior and so now I just have to wait because he's going to be the big
> money maker. I just have to kind of wait.

This plan to prioritize being in the same location and waiting for the male
to make his decision was predominant for these six women.

Four of the interviewees had boyfriends during college, but they expressed that this had been "just a college thing. He's just not driven." These
young women said that it had been important to have a boyfriend in college
but that they knew that the particular person whom they were dating was
not a good choice for them to marry. However, even though Samantha, one
of these four, recognized the lack of drive in her boyfriend, she still seemed
to be struggling with maintaining this relationship:

> Right now, school's my life so that's what I talk about and that's what I
> discuss. Sometimes he thinks I guess I neglect him . . . which is why I don't
> talk about it all the time. . . . but sometimes he feels like I'm condescend-
> ing. It's getting better. I try to be careful about it. It's not a major problem.

The other seven students told me that they had not dated much during
college. They thought that dating would be a "distraction" and that they
had to focus on their schoolwork. When Tracy was asked about romance in
her life, she told me,

> It's like you can't win. You know you really can't do what you really want
> to do. I mean you may not be as successful in a career as you want to be
> just because you're a woman . . . although it's changing. But at the same
> time, if you decide to be a wife and mother as well as, or only, then people
> think that you've just given away your life. And I don't know.

Although more research would be necessary to make definitive statements about the place of romantic relationships, the students who described
relationships built on mutuality may have been operating from fourth-order

thinking. These learners spent some time explaining the ways in which the couple had discussed their future plan and how they weighed each other's goals when making their final decision. The women arranging their lives around their boyfriends' plans appear to be operating from a relational/transitional mode. The attachment to their boyfriend and meeting his needs appears to define their "selves." It could be that maintaining this romantic interest provided them with a degree of certainty when approaching the uncertain, open-endedness of leaving the college environment. In contrast, those women who had maintained a dating relationship during college, but now recognized that they had different needs, might have been progressing to the point of realizing that they could author and meet their own needs. However, it seemed that they had wanted someone to date at school, perhaps for security or perhaps to fit in with the culture. The last group appears to be committed to academics and, thus, not interested in pursuing a romantic attachment. For these young women, some may have been operating from a self-authored position, or they may have been struggling with the balance of connection and autonomy, unable yet to imagine that a relationship might support self-authorship rather than consume their own sense of independence. It is important to note that this analysis is not an attempt to dismiss the importance of romantic relationships but rather perhaps to illuminate whether these relationships, or lack thereof, constitute decisions made from a position of a self-authored identity, from the position of needing to meet external expectations, or from the idea that the relationship defines the "self." All 20 of these young women discussed the role of heterosexual, romantic relationships as an area of concern going into their future. Another type of relationship also dominated these interviews, an analysis of family members.

Family Members

Regardless of whether these women stated that they were very close, somewhat close, or not really close to their families, each of them had much to say about the personalities of their mothers, fathers, stepparents, and siblings. Nine of these young women described very close relationships with their parents, especially their mothers, referring to them as "my best friend." These learners analyzed their parents' behavior and expressed concern about what their parents needed. Hannah worried about her mother being lonely: "I wish she had more peers her age to interact with." Hannah's mother was divorced and had to raise two girls by herself. Hannah said, "I am really proud of my mom. I admire so much what she has been able to do." She had also noticed that her younger sister "is much stronger" than she is: "She has this boyfriend who keeps messing with her and she can just lay it on the line. I can't really do that." Carol also described her parents as "friends," but, she said, "I still know that I can call on them and say, 'OK, don't be my friend, be my parent and tell me what I need to do.'" Carol also felt very close to her two sisters, saying that she felt she had to be a "role model for them." She worried about the fact that her sisters cried whenever she left from a visit to return to school, and she knew that her family missed her but were at the same time very supportive and proud. These women appeared to empathize with their families and wanted to give back to them. Their relationships with their families seemed to be part of their self-identity and dictated some of their choices and decisions. They all expressed concern that they "not disappoint" their family.

Six students described relationships with their family that might be categorized as somewhat close. They discussed their family relationships, indicating that they still "love [their] parents and they are supportive," but also mentioned the fact that they felt they had separated from their need to be constantly in touch. Mary's comments expressed that sentiment best:

> I think it's difficult for [my father]. He doesn't know when to stop being that parent that is able to . . . he thinks to be a parent . . . you tell them what they should do and they do what you tell them and he has a problem realizing that I'm an adult now. [Because] I don't have to live with him anymore then obviously his advice or whatever doesn't mean anything. . . . I think that his problem . . . it's more how to be a parent after your kids are grown.

The analysis of these six women seemed more objective than that of the previous group. For example, Jasmine said that her parents "just keep very busy": "My dad just wants to make sure I can support myself. He doesn't want me to live off of him and I don't want to." Debbie described her mother as "very controlling" and her father as "in a very different space now." When Beth told her mother that she had changed her major from pre-med to English, she noted that her mother's reaction seemed negative. Beth's conversation revealed an ability to step back and analyze the motives for her mother's reaction:

[Mom's] really big—because my parents are separated—she's really big on like women supporting themselves, things like that, 'cause she kind of comes from a generation of, you know, divorce. Some of the women make it and some of them don't depending on if they have a career. And I understand that, and believe it too, but I think she was hoping for something more concrete for me to do.

These women seemed able to maintain their own decisions and did not mention disappointing their parents. It could be that they were beginning to be able to reflect on their relationships and did not feel that they needed to give up their choices in order to please their families.

The third group of women described relationships with their families that did not appear to be close ones. These five students mentioned that their parents were supportive but that they did not visit or communicate with them very often. Nancy described an argument with her father, saying he was just "pushing and pushing": "I get so frustrated because neither of them [her parents] . . . went to college and I'm like, you have no idea what it's like." These students seemed to have separated from their families, even saying, "they're concerned about their own things right now." All these women labeled themselves "very independent, and they [their families] know it." They seemed to operate from their own goals and needs; as Lesa said, "I do what I want. I would never stay someplace just to please someone else." It is difficult to ascertain from the dialogue whether these students operated from a position of self-authorship or one of simply meeting their own needs and wants, but with little reflection on the reasons for their choices.

All these young women spent time discussing romantic and family relationships, with varying degrees of involvement. Each one said that she hoped she would be married with children at some point, some sooner than others. They all described futures that sounded like middle-class, suburban life. The future and what it might hold was a strong topic of discussion. For most of them, however, discussing their friends created the strongest emotional responses.

The Role of Friends

Of the interviewed women, only one mentioned the fact that she discussed what she had learned in classes with her friends. The majority of them said that they talk to their friends about "life"—stress, pressure, relationships, the future, and their personalities. In fact, every student mentioned talking about when they "get out of school, what it's going to be like." In addition, many of these women said that they talked with their friends about "balancing family and work." They seemed to struggle with the expectation that women need to "do it all." Tracy said that she loved talking with her roommate "for 3 or 4 hours at a time": "We talk about parking problems, which will work into feminism which will work into how horrible the world is and just all these things." Most of these students said that leaving their friends was the hardest part of graduating.

For Carol, her college experience taught her "what true friendship is": "These are people who accept me for who I am which gives me the courage to be who I am." Mary noted that it was a good experience to have all of her friends around her to talk with "because we are all going through this together." For these students, being surrounded by peers, others who could empathize with the college experience, "made college what it is."

It is interesting that these women did not analyze the personalities of their friends in the same way that they evaluated their family members or their boyfriends. Perhaps as their development evolved, they could sense a self that was separate from their families and, sometimes, from romantic partners, but their friends appeared to be an extension of their identity. It may be that individuals, rather than move all their relationships to objects of study at one time, slowly separate themselves from others. Given that these friends seem to be experiencing the same life changes and choices at the same time, it may be that viewing these friends as external to the self is a slower process. These women still seemed to be quite embedded in their friendships as they considered the next move to the "real world."

The Real World Versus School

All the women in our study discussed the "real world" as very separate from "school." One student felt that life outside college was so different that she feared she might discover "that school might be the only thing [she's] good at." Debbie talked about being scared to graduate because she felt that she had never had the opportunity to make her own decisions:

> All I know is people telling me what to do and now I'm having to tell myself what to do. They make you live in a dorm. They control where you

live, where you eat, what you do and, yeah, I think college is a very controlling place. I'm scared that [college] hasn't really prepared me for the real
world.

The majority of the women said, "I just want to get my life started."
Many of them described class as "irrelevant to my life" or "just task oriented." Several expressed that they hoped their real lives were not like school,
constantly filled with "go, go, go and do, do, do." The women discussed
feeling constant stress in their college lives. Anna presented the following
description of student life:

> You have to be involved, so then they [students] try to get involved, and
> then they have all their school work and they try to do all their school work
> and I think a good part of college, or whatever, it's not really the school,
> but you're just out there experiencing, and you're finding out who you
> want to be, who you are, what you want to do, and I think that has more
> to do with it than school. But a lot of it is grades, grades, grades, and
> involvement; because you know you've always got to get the perfect job
> and stuff like that. I think it's just a lot of pressure and a lot of stress and
> I think it just gets to be too much.

This statement suggests that, for students, schoolwork resembles errands, or
housework: things to complete so that enjoyable and meaningful activities
can follow. This disconnect between school and the "real world" might
imply that assignments in classes appear irrelevant to students' lives; in addition, the context in which class material is presented may seem removed
from what students perceive to be important: knowing themselves and what
the future holds. Even though these comments sound discouraging, however, these young women did claim that they had learned much during their
college experience.

When these young women discussed what they had learned during college, none of them discussed specific content or even her major discipline.
Instead, they suggested that classes had taught them to think, "reason things
out," and "question everything." Almost half of these learners mentioned
becoming more "open-minded and tolerant" due to exposure to different
cultures. Jenny indicated when the most significant learning occurred: when
classes "threw me into different circumstances, where I had to figure out

what I thought." Tracy explained when she felt the most challenged by her classes:

> [when they help me] think a lot about our value system and the way we look at [things] and that got me thinking about the way I look at life and integrity a lot. It made me think about what values I hold up highly and let me think in terms of other classes. . . . Made me think outside the box and . . . think of people and not just ourselves and our own college experience and makes us think of how we can affect other people.

These comments suggest that learning was strongest when it helped students determine their own sense of identity. The students described their new knowledge not in some separate abstract way but rather in relation to the changes that they experienced in their vision of themselves.

Another classroom feature that many students discussed involved the opportunity to listen to other students and to have open conversations. Many of the women said that they learned by listening and "hearing about other people's choices." Jasmine suggested that she was finding her voice when she stated, "I am much more outgoing now, because I have learned to voice my opinion and people listen."

These women, however, indicated that their out-of-class experiences provided the strongest learning environments. Four of the students had studied abroad for a semester, but it was not the immersion in another culture that dominated their discussion about their travels but rather the fact that they were away from "friends, family, and everything familiar." These students indicated that it was during this time that they learned "to rely on" themselves. This separation from their relatives and peers gave them "self-confidence" and a chance to "be [themselves]."

Internships and off-campus jobs also provided the women with valuable learning experiences. They noted that this was the only way that they could "know how things really work." Erin described the significance of her work experiences:

> Some people just stay in the . . . school. You can be the smartest person alive and it's not going to matter when you get out in the real world. You might be able to quote some . . . rule, but that's not going to help you when are trying to explain it to somebody. [Work] helps me keep that perspective on keeping things simple for trying to communicate to that person if they don't understand everything exactly as you do.

These learners suggested that classes were for learning concrete facts and laws but that the more important aspect would be the ability to communicate with different kinds of people, not just faculty and other students.

Being involved in student organizations and activities also promoted a sense of learning. Terri said that by being in cheerleading she learned to "set [her] own goals and challenge [herself] better than in class." Erin discussed working on the yearbook and realizing that she "learned that some people are very creative, but they need some other types of people. I think we value [all] sides because it takes everyone." Carol was involved in several activities during her time in college and described when she began to see herself as a "role model": "when other students came up to me and said, 'I know you. You are in——organization.' This gave me self-confidence." Many of these traits are presented in certain classes, but it seemed that having the opportunity to experience the application of these characteristics gave students a stronger sense of learning than discussing and reading about them.

Three of the women experienced their parents' divorce during college. They actually credited that experience as the strongest factor in their personal growth. Each of them indicated that this event made them "grow up and face reality," as they realized that "things don't always go as you plan them. There are no 'rose colored' glasses." One of these students sought counseling on campus, but all three of them said that their friends were the ones who actually helped them with their emotional reactions and disillusionment; as Wendy said, "They [her friends] were my lifesavers. They taught me to go on and focus on school. I can't imagine life without them." Peer support remained crucial to their success as students.

One factor that many of the women felt was missing from their college experience was "time to reflect, just think about things." Anna described her "epiphany" on a spring break trip, indicating a possible shift to fourth-order/ independent thinking:

> I was laying out on the beach, my roommate was beside me; we weren't talking or anything, just cut off from everyone. You know, sun beating down on me, feeling just like, just thinking about things. I just realized . . . that I don't really care too much about what people think of me because . . . that was one of the big things that I was holding back and maybe that's why I was always stressed out. I don't want to change myself any more to please other people. If [other students] are kind of like me . . . and trying

to just blend in . . . I think eventually . . . they'll realize . . . "what am I doing? Why did I all of a sudden become this person instead of myself?"

As these seniors discussed their lives at school, the majority said they wished they had taken time to reflect on the changes that had happened to them along the way. However, their number-one comment was, "There's so much stress and I am so busy all the time." It is not clear whether the amount of class work created this feeling of stress or whether students filled their days with other tasks and work until there was not enough time to get everything done. Regardless of the cause, all the women felt that their lives involved "a lot of pressure."

What Does This Mean and What Can We Do?

Overall, the students in our study seemed to present three overarching themes: (a) struggling with a sense of pressure to get everything done, (b) seeking a balance between autonomy and connection, and (c) coping with the realization of the uncertainty of the future. Some people may say that the college experience presents individuals with the chance to simply live life, free of the worries about mortgages, jobs, children, and other responsibilities. The students in our study did not echo this view. It sounded as if every moment was filled with tasks to be completed, places to be, things to accomplish. Their voices appeared to affirm the feeling of being subject to external demands at the expense of their own sense of self-designed lives. These students might benefit from knowing that on the other side of the bridge exists the chance to create your own life, set your own goals, and establish a self-directed set of values and priorities. However, it is not enough for them simply to be aware of this fact; institutions of higher education can create systematic opportunities for students to engage in some of these tasks throughout their years in school. Academic advising offers an opportunity for initiating this approach. Creating a system in which advisers ask students to set goals and respond periodically to questions that ask them to reflect on their values and priorities could begin this process of transformation. However, such a system requires investing in people committed to undertaking this responsibility. If an institution uses faculty as advisers, then this function must be supported with release time and sufficient assistance. If colleges and universities employ professional advisers, then the number of advisees assigned to each person must be reasonable. Unfortunately, in times of budget constraints, academic advising rarely receives the funding it deserves. More research demonstrating the possible benefits of enhancing advising systems could encourage stronger financial support for this function.

In the classroom, faculty might also encourage more self-directed endeavors through problem-based learning, individualized assignments, and student-designed sections of the course. These initiatives, however, need to be supported by the institution. Rethinking faculty workloads and the criteria for promotion and tenure that allow these changes would need to be addressed.

Balancing the tension between autonomy and connection is a lifelong process. Far too often the two appear as dualistic choices. Although Kegan (1982) assures his readers that "autonomy" can be inclusive of relationships, for many women, "autonomy" tends to signal aloneness. Transitional learners tend to be unaware that on the other side of the bridge, individuals develop the ability to choose and construct their relationships, as well as the confidence to voice their own needs and wants. Often students attend presentations on such topics as "Healthy Relationships," but these do not give students experiences that allow them to engage in this transformation. These learners need to know that this tension between the self and relationships is not a zero-sum game but rather that connections to others can produce growth in all parties in the relationship (Jordan, Kaplan, Miller, Stiver, & Surrey, 1991).

In order to enhance students' understanding of the importance and centrality of relationships, some people have suggested that college women and men be given more responsibility for the culture (Belenky, Bond, & Weinstock, 1997). Rather than create reactive rules, institutions of higher education could engage students in ownership of the environment, both physical and emotional, at their schools. Whether it be responsibility for their own housing unit, departmental functions, college activities and buildings, or specific rules and regulations of student life, if students work together to create their own living space from a sense of responsibility, perhaps it would encourage them to develop a deeper understanding of and appreciation for the place of relationships in their lives. Another recommendation is that students maintain close relationships with their parents, especially their mothers and other female role models (Dooley & Fedele, 2004). However, educators need to assist students in having adult relationships with their parents, so that they will experience growth in an evolving connection. A third suggestion is that more opportunities be made available for students to form support groups, some designed around discussions of issues, others around active projects. This could help learners recognize the role of interdependency, as well as support the idea that working with and caring for others is not a weakness but rather a requirement of adult life.

Within the classroom, attention can be brought to the interplay between the affective and cognitive elements of meaning making. Often educators attempt to separate these two domains, partly because Western culture supports this division. However, some women, and men, do not make meaning in this compartmentalized fashion. In fact, findings from neuroscience suggest that the affective domain is instrumental to the learning process (Johnson & Taylor, 2006). Discussions that ask students to reflect on their own values, relationships, and beliefs, as well as respond to differing perspectives, might help teach students to navigate difference and conflict while maintaining relationships. Having multiple opportunities for different relationships may help these learners as they struggle with accepting uncertainty.

The women in our study all expressed concern about making decisions in an uncertain world. Such concerns validate the work of Kegan (1982) and Baxter Magolda (1992), for it appears that these learners were moving into the world of independent knowing and fourth-order thinking. In order for students to become more comfortable with uncertainty, they must be encouraged to take some reasonable risks. Engaging in internships, community work, and study abroad could all provide experiences that have elements of uncertainty but also offer opportunities that should provide successful outcomes. To further the internalization of these ventures, and to encourage students to recognize how these opportunities truly are uncertain adventures, intentional reflection activities should accompany these experiences. These could be written assignments or presentations to other students. The process of reflection serves as an anchoring device, as well as providing students with a way to connect these activities with what they are learning and who they are becoming.

There are institutions that have implemented many of these suggestions and more; there is also evidence that these practices create a healthier climate for women (Wolf-Wendel, 2000). Will this address some of the issues presented earlier in this chapter, specifically the pressure on women to pursue heterosexual relationships at the cost of their academic focus, the prevalence of sexual harassment, and the encouragement to consume excessive amounts of alcohol? This question leads to a broader set of questions about the purpose of higher education.

Concluding Remarks

As a caveat, this study consisted of a small sample of only women from a homogeneous student population at a small institution in the Midwest. As with any qualitative study, these results are not meant to be generalizable. Given the latest reports on sexual harassment and excessive drinking on campuses, however, I hope that these findings will encourage more research and action. Many institutions may have action plans that address the issues in this chapter, but this investigation points out some disconnects between students' out-of-class experience and the experience we hope for them. In addition, this chapter raises broad questions about the role of higher education in societal development.

Some people may declare that the purpose of higher education is to "educate" and that institutions of higher education are not responsible for these more "personal issues." However, if Kegan (1994) is correct in stating that modern life demands fourth-order thinking, then it appears that helping students to move toward more complex ways of knowing must be a requirement for colleges and universities, if, as most mission statements claim, we seek to educate citizens equipped to live in a democracy and to engage in lifelong learning. Baxter Magolda and King (2004) assert that assisting students in their cognitive development requires starting where they are and helping them across the bridge of development. These researchers declare that students, for the most part, enter college embedded in their relationships and their need for belonging. It seems reasonable that these learners would agree to follow the cultural norms in order to maintain their sense of self.

In the interviews in our study, students appeared to struggle with a perception of stress and pressure, an enhanced involvement with analyzing relationships, and uncertainty about the future. Kegan (1994) notes that fostering development requires intentional intervention. He questions whether leaving young adults to find their own way places the full responsibility on those most unequipped to move themselves forward. If all students could engage in setting their own goals, assuming ownership for the physical and cultural environment of the college or university, and pursuing and reflecting on experiences that provide success in dealing with uncertainty, perhaps the culture on campus could change. If these young women, and men, see faculty and staff celebrating and encouraging these activities, maybe their initial stage of learning the culture could be different. In the current state of the world, encouraging young adults to assume responsibility for creating a world grounded in supporting and sustaining cultures that promote self-authored interdependency appears to be a need and a source of hope.

References

Allen, J. K., & Taylor, K. (2006). The senior year transition: Women college undergraduates search for a path. *Journal of College Student Development, 47*(6), 595–608.

Baxter Magolda, M. B. (1992). *Knowing and reasoning in college: Gender-related patterns in students' intellectual development.* San Francisco: Jossey-Bass.

Baxter Magolda, M. B., & King, P. M. (Eds.). (2004). *Learning partnerships: Theory and models of practice to educate for self-authorship.* Sterling, VA: Stylus.

Belenky, M. F., Bond, L. A., & Weinstock, J. S. (1997). *A tradition that has no name: Nurturing the development of people, families, and communities.* New York: Basic Books.

Belenky, M. F., Clinchy, B. M., Goldberger, N. R., & Tarule, J. M. (1986). *Women's ways of knowing: The development of self, voice, and mind.* New York: Basic Books.

Dooley, C., & Fedele, N. (2004). Mothers and sons: Raising relational boys. In J. V. Jordan, M. Walker, & L. M. Hartling (Eds.), *The complexity of connection: Writings from the Stone Center's Jean Baker Miller Training Institute* (pp. 220–249). New York: Guilford Press.

Elkins, B., Helms, L. B., & Pierson, C. T. (2003). Greek-letter organizations, alcohol, and the courts: A risky mix? *Journal of College Student Development, 44*(1), 67–80.

Gmelch, S. B. (1998). *Gender on campus: Issues for college women.* New Brunswick, NJ: Rutgers University Press.

Hall, R. M., & Sandler, B. R. (1984). *Out of the classroom: A chilly campus climate for women?* Washington, DC: Association of American Colleges.

Hill, C., & Silva, E. (2005). *Drawing the line: Sexual harassment on campus.* Washington, DC: American Association of University Women Educational Foundation.

Holland, D. C., & Eisenhart, M. A. (1990). *Educated in romance: Women, achievement, and college culture.* Chicago: University of Chicago Press.

Johnson, S., & Taylor, K. (Eds.). (2006). *New Directions for Adult and Continuing Education, Vol. 110: The neuroscience of adult learning.* San Francisco: Jossey-Bass.

Jordan, J. V., Kaplan, A. G., Miller, J. B., Stiver, I. P., & Surrey, J. L. (1991). *Women's growth in connection: Writings from the Stone Center.* New York: Guilford Press.

Josselson, R. (1996). *Revising herself: The story of women's identity from college to midlife.* New York: Oxford University Press.

Kaly, P. W., Heesacker, M., & Frost, H. M. (2002). Collegiate alcohol use and high-risk sexual behavior: A literature review. *Journal of College Student Development, 43*(6), 838–850.

Kegan, R. (1982). *The evolving self: Problem and process in human development.* Cambridge, MA: Harvard University Press.

Kegan, R. (1994). *In over our heads: The mental demands of modern life.* Cambridge, MA: Harvard University Press.

Love, P. G., & Guthrie, V. L. (1999). *New Directions for Student Services: Vol. 88. Understanding and applying cognitive development theory.* San Francisco: Jossey-Bass.

Newell, M. (Writer), & Goldsmith-Thomas, E., Schindler, D., and Schiff, P. (Producers). (2004). *Mona Lisa smile* [Motion picture]. United States: Columbia Pictures.

Perry, W. G. (1970). *Forms of intellectual and ethical development in the college years: A scheme.* Troy, MO: Holt, Rinehart & Winston.

Wolf-Wendel, L. E. (2000). Women-friendly campuses: What five institutions are doing right. *Review of Higher Education, 23*(3), 319–345.

8

SUBMERGED FEMINISM(S)?

Perceptions of Adult Education Student Experiences With Women's Studies Scholarship

Susan J. Bracken

Women's studies has often been characterized as both an academic discipline and a social movement. For 19 years I have worked in universities and also been involved in women's studies. I have followed with great personal and professional interest debates about what directions women's studies should go next. Several years ago, I made a transition from my role as a full-time member of a women's studies program and department with part-time participation in adult and higher education to the inverse: I became a full-time member of the adult and higher education disciplinary community with part-time women's studies or feminist participation. This change put me into a state of questioning about what I see happening in my home disciplines and beyond. This chapter is a preliminary discussion of the questions that I have raised with myself, my students, and my colleagues about the nature of women's studies and adult education praxis. It explores my perception of adult education students' movement toward submerged forms of feminist work, and of an increasing focus on public, individual selves and less of a focus on collective feminist identities.

What Do the Fields of Adult Education and Women's Studies Have in Common?

Adult education is a graduate field of study and an area of practice that is often misunderstood. Most of the scholars with whom I interact associate it with the study of adult basic education and literacy or some form of education directed at "bringing adults up to speed." Although this is a major area of study within the field, there are many other areas of study and practice that are important to know about. Adult education frames adult life experiences as *learning experiences,* and from that position it studies the many sociocultural, political, technical and instrumental, cognitive and psychological ways that adults can learn or help others to learn. It places special emphasis on adult learning with the goal of stimulating positive social change. This work takes place in a range of contexts from grassroots or community education to formal postsecondary returning adult students. As such, the field of adult education studies social movement learning, the experiences and nature of adult learning, all aspects of university continuing and distance education efforts (which are primarily dedicated to adult learners), adult learners in postsecondary institutions, and other types of formal and informal learning in nonprofit centers, community action groups, schools, and workplace organizations. The majority of graduate students in adult education programs are also actively working in some other form of adult education—as activists, educational leaders, nonprofit directors, continuing education specialists, teachers, facilitators, human resources directors, policy analysts—or they are looking for a way to make a career change to one of these settings. Nearly all of them navigate an interesting irony: they themselves are returning adult learners whose chosen field of study involves the examination of adult learning experiences. Thus, they have to make meaning of what they are studying as something that is directly relevant to their own lived experiences.

With that basic description in mind, and allowing that there are notable disciplinary differences that will not be discussed in this chapter, adult education shares at least six important characteristics with the field of women's studies:

1. A commitment to study and action surrounding issues of social equity, equality, diversity, access and social participation, and the role that values and culture play in our lives
2. An explicit overlap between the curriculum and a central part of the student's identity: adult learners studying adult learning and women's studies students studying the role of gender in their lives

3. A commitment to the principle of praxis, the idea that scholarship and theory cannot be cleanly separated from practice, and vice versa, and that engagement is critical to this mutual process
4. A relatively young presence within the academy and at times intense internal debate about what future directions should or could be
5. A healthy tension between desires for disciplinarity and interdisciplinarity
6. A vision of nature and purpose that is sometimes seen as skewed or incomplete by those outside the discipline

In this chapter, I discuss my perception of issues that commonly surface as adult education graduate students learn about gender and women's studies. I then use the discussion of these issues as a vehicle for framing new questions and creating future conversations about contemporary disciplinary issues within both disciplines.

Reflections on Adult Education Students' Learning About Women's and Gender Studies

Most adult education students are working full-time adult learners pursuing graduate school on a part-time basis. They have considerable life experience with adult relationships and with personal, civic, and work responsibilities, and they are highly motivated to learn and to connect their learning to their respective environments. A small subgroup of students are full-time students or are pursuing academic careers as future faculty members, with the majority preparing for professional positions external to universities and colleges. Many students exposed to feminist frameworks express appreciation for the rich contributions of women's studies scholarship external to adult education and to feminist scholarship within adult education in several key areas. First, they grasp and seek out publications centered on the roles that ontology, axiology, and epistemology play in understanding adult learning, education, and life experiences. They also often comment on, choose, and apply readings from feminist literature regarding research study design, implementation, and interpretation, particularly qualitative research. Adult education pedagogical principles emphasize the development of learner voice, participatory teaching, and facilitation approaches and promote analysis of the role of power and culture in educative processes. As a result, students often utilize feminist pedagogical scholarship as a resource for their own work, even when it is not directly gender focused. Finally, students interested in diversity studies and the role that culture and values play in learning and community engagement draw heavily on feminist work within and outside adult education.

In spite of these parallels, there are some points of concern in the way adult education students sometimes respond to and engage with feminist scholarship. The remainder of this section presents a brief discussion of those patterns, and the final section discusses the broader implications and suggests questions for the future.

Submerged Feminism/Feminist(s)?

The topic of "I am not a feminist, but . . ." is one that has been explored in the feminist literature for quite some time (Hall & Salupo Rodriguez, 2003; Nelson, Shanahan & Olivetti, 1997; Ouellette, 1992). It can take many forms, but the gist of the argument is that many people, in this case students, often express agreement with the goals of the women's movement, with egalitarian ideals and women's equality, but do not want to be identified or associated with the "f" words: feminist and feminism. This phenomenon is something I encounter regularly in my adult education teaching, research, and practice and something that also occurred in my previous women's studies environments.

For some students, this phenomenon appears to stem from incomplete or erroneous information about what feminism is, and as students learn more, they become more comfortable with identifying with or using the language associated with feminism. In a manner that resembles Boxer's (1998) discussion of the phase theory of women's studies curriculum, students also go through stages of understanding the complexities and levels of feminist work that may inform their academic interest areas. According to Boxer, using McIntosh's example of the study of history, the five phases represent a continuum: "womanless history; women in history; women as a problem; anomaly or absence in history; women as history; and, history reconstructed or redefined to include us all" (Boxer, 1998, p. 62). Along similar lines, scholars have described the formation of feminist consciousness: Often it begins with the recognition of the mistreatment of women on an individual experiential level. Next is a reframing of individual acts of mistreatment or unfairness to a big-picture view, relabeling individual problems with individual forms of redress to social or shared issues that warrant collective or shared solutions (Klatch, 2001).

On the other hand, a growing proportion of our students seem to want to walk the line and draw increasingly on feminist scholarship yet dissociate from the terms *feminist* and *feminism(s)* for a few core reasons. The first is the argument that students simply do not want to adopt a label that they believe will cause professional or personal discomfort or harm or even jeopardize their abilities to gain employment. Many of them are vocal in asserting that they understand and have considered the implications of taking this position. On this basis, a few choose specialty areas that explicitly disconnect from an area of scholarship and practice (feminist) that they consider important and valuable but personally unsafe. More often, students interested in feminism who reject public identification as feminist scholars relay that they would prefer to do "good work" (in relation to gender) without feeling a need for a collective identity or label. They describe their issues of congruence or salience to be connected to a specific issue such as women's learning, women's access to higher education, community health, and so on. If asked, these students deny their affiliation with feminism or feminist studies. Or they sometimes claim an interest in "diversity issues" but reject stronger terms such as *social change, social justice, feminism,* and *activism.* This strategy becomes increasingly difficult as students struggle to reference and attribute their scholarly writing appropriately to sources that are clearly identified as feminist. This hesitancy has far-reaching consequences for remembering and furthering the contributions that academic feminism makes to the academy. The strategy also grows difficult as students' work and identities become more integrated.

A third compromise strategy is to "do" feminist scholarship openly and avoid the label in titles, names of projects, and personal identification, in the hope that others do not make the association of their gender studies with feminism. Students who choose this path are confident, at least during their graduate-student phase, that their two worlds will not collide and that they can go about their studies in a parallel universe of sorts. As a fourth strategy, students who are supportive and interested in feminist scholarship and practice will often openly study and write from a feminist perspective but studiously avoid the label *feminist* when discussing or presenting their work to their external adult education practice areas.[1] These students describe their choice as a political one that they believe will increase or enhance their practical effectiveness.

Finally, as a fifth strategy, some students who are doing feminist work appear to be uncertain about whether they will be able to sustain their work in this area. They express resistance to notions of doing "emotional labor." Barbara Omolade's (2002) discussion of women's studies and class issues within the classroom conveys the importance of understanding "emotional labor." She argues that working women experience multiple aspects of class and that analysis needs to rest within women's voices and experiences and not necessarily within ideology or structures alone. She further states that many of her students who are working class mistakenly self-identify as middle-class because of their presence in the classroom and the fact that they are neither poverty stricken nor wealthy. Building on the work of Hochschild and of Steinberg and Figart, Omolade (2002) defines emotional labor as the relational rather than task work involved in certain types of jobs, and she describes it as a critical and often ignored contributor to work, especially service work. She further discusses how certain positions or work situations entail sustained contact with others and require the management or suppression of strong or complex emotions in order to influence or benefit others. Omolade points out that women engaged in emotional labor often report that others do not realize how emotionally draining certain types of work can be.

Building on Omolade's work, I believe that a portion of adult education students foresee the difficulties involved with making a professional and personal choice that involves large amounts of emotional labor and that their decision to avoid feminist work is based on this rationale. Such a decision is not always easy, as students describe feeling a definite pull toward feminist or other types of social justice study and view it as a barrier to a less demanding life path. A former student, Gloria[2] describes it this way:

> I understand and even feel pulled towards the articles we read in class that discuss social justice and the importance of adopting critical perspectives in adult education, . . . but I also hit a point where I don't want to be responsible for anything else. I want to be sensitive to diversity, to gender, race, class, . . . but I'm not really an activist. I am already juggling work, school, and taking care of my family, and it is enough. I am passionate about my work and have moments where I don't think I am able to set

personal boundaries and avoid emotional turmoil. I hear examples in class of how to integrate critical perspectives into action, but in my day-to-day life I get nervous. . . . I love the idea of changing the world. I'm just not sure of the personal and emotional cost.

The concept of emotional labor is further complicated by many adult education students' desire to study the intersections of gender, class, race, and sexual orientation. Many of them report that they attempt to enter poststructural or other areas of feminist scholarship in an attempt to integrate their inquiry, and they are overwhelmed and confused about how to study multiple dimensions of identity at the same time.

Taken together, these students could be viewed as engaging in submerged feminism(s). They are actively engaged in strategies that submerge their feminist leanings, yet they attempt to preserve feminist work, ideals, and social change. For some scholars this duality is untenable, but for others their feminist identities are internalized and public identification is not viewed as necessary.

The Personal Is Political . . . Has the Political Also Become Personal?

One of the cornerstones of feminist pedagogy and of adult education is placing a value on experience as a source of learning and understanding and on the development of voice (Hayes & Flannery, 2000). Overall, both fields promote and encourage the use of dialogue, biography, autoethnography, and narrative as forms of scholarly expression regarding women's lives. A challenge that the adult education field has faced is the historical predominance of adult learning theories and frameworks that are overly individualistic or based too heavily on psychological explanations of adult learning and experience (Cunningham, 2000). The challenge is in balancing this critique with the simultaneous desire for forms of participatory learning and narrative scholarship and practice. Further, there are remarkable advances in the application of technology as a tool for feminist (and all forms) of instruction and research; more than ever we see video, audio, photographic, and other forms of information that capture "experience" as a part of our work.

The slogan *the personal is political,* as four small words, has had tremendous power and impact on the women's movement and on feminist scholarship. It has many layers of meaning, and I draw on it as a reminder that an individual inequity or injustice is something that is of concern to all of us. In the process of solving a problem, we are reminded that there are often systemic or structural explanations and solutions for seemingly individual situations. The phrase also serves as an important reminder that issues that seem to be outside our own identities cannot be cleanly set apart from feminist work—a commitment to gender equality therefore also signifies a corresponding commitment to other types of social equality. As adult education students study feminist work, many of them tend to gravitate to pedagogical discussions because they are complementary to adult education pedagogical discussions and also because of a comfort level with education and the educative process associated with individual empowerment. The journey of self-discovery through studying something that is deeply meaningful and personal has a seductive appeal and feels hugely valuable. A language of reflection, reflection and action, reflective practice, participatory action, and participation situates the "I" as a major actor within the "we" or "us." Even seemingly straightforward and collective agendas (such as improving female adult learner access to higher education) are often based on arguments about the individual benefits and experiences of educational attainment. And as narrative inquiry and applications of narrative inquiry grow, many students are uncritically adopting a "personal story" approach to their scholarship. The consequence of these well-meaning approaches is a fragmented identity politics and an incomplete scholarship and practice base. This outcome leads to my questioning of whether the discourse in adult education, or perhaps the discourse of social movements, has moved away from "the personal is political" and adopted a stance that the political is personal. In doing so, feminist studies within adult education might well be an example of what it is to develop and exercise power while concurrently diminishing one's power. I am not suggesting that we abandon or reduce our focus on narrative inquiry or on women's experiences as sources of understanding but that we should be careful to examine critically our engagement with this type of learning and expression.

In an odd sort of way, the political has become personal in discussions of the future directions of the adult education discipline. There have been many recurring discussions about the central purpose of the field and the tensions between those who prefer social justice and social movement learning and those who prefer organizational modes of adult education (adult basic education, continuing education, and the like). These discussions are often tied to discussions of the field's survival and future success within the academy. Weber's interpretation of social action groups as going through a dynamic phase and then collapsing or conforming to the larger environment is certainly similar to some of the arguments about the forces that adult education (as a field) faces and the choices it will have to make in order to sustain a successful academic identity without losing its grassroots social justice roots. In other words, many people believe that the arc of development of the discipline of adult education is at a crossroads and that it is imperative to negotiate the next pathway thoughtfully (Welton, 1987; Wilson & Hayes, 2000).

Renewed Understanding of Adult Education and Women's Studies as Social Movements and Academic Disciplines

Stepping back, one of the important ways that we can attempt to understand contemporary adult education students' reactions and pathways with feminist scholarship is to reconsider the larger picture. Within both fields, faculty members and students participate within and beyond the academy as scholar-activists or as members of academic social movements.[3] Essentially, our students by virtue of their student status are participants in a social movement, though some may not identify in this way. Thus, changes in research and in creating new conceptualizations of social movements may lend a hand in understanding corresponding changes or dilemmas within our disciplinary contexts. There are two connected ideas that are especially useful in setting up future discussions of praxis and in increasing our understanding of cultural shifts in our students and future faculty members. They are (1) the exploration of a conceptual shift from collective identity to other forms of organizing and (2) the exploration of the culture of "public self" through narration.

Exploration of a Cultural Shift from Collective Identity to Other Forms of Organizing

My discussion of operating concepts of social movements centers around life experiences with collective identity and solidarity. McDonald (2002) discusses the possibility of exploring social movements as reflections of larger changes in societal culture, with increased consumerism, individualism, and social practices. He traces the earlier split between an "identity" and a "strategy" approach to social movements evidenced in the sociology social movement literature during the 1980s. According to McDonald (2002), this split was followed by a 1990s emphasis on the integration of identity and strategy; in fact, identity itself became a resource to be strategically mobilized. This shift was mirrored by the move from a banking theory of education to one that constructs the self as a narrator, connecting education to life experiences. McDonald's view supports work by Alberto Melucci, who suggests that collective identity then took on an instrumental definition and that the sense of community and solidarity can be diminished as a result. Other scholars explore contemporary interpretations of community and identity and argue that the decline of a sense of community is leading to largely individualistic cultural attitudes, behaviors, and belief systems. McDonald suggests that there is an increase in the formation of *affinity groups,* a term used to describe small, temporary social action groups that form specific short-term goals, work together to achieve those goals, and subsequently disband. Members of affinity groups are not going through a process of developing feminist (or other) consciousness; they are coming together because of a shared agenda such as saving a park or increasing pay equity in a particular time/place/organization. Self-discovery and meaning making are not critical elements of an affinity group experience, although arguably they could happen. Another element of affinity groups is their present-day focus (short term), as opposed to a focus on the long-term future.

What is the significance of this shift away from collective identity? Certainly at some level, these ideas run at least partially parallel to concepts of third-wave feminism (Baumgardner & Richards, 2000) and stir up images and remembrances of tensions among feminists about the value of collectivity and the value of individual expression within social movements, in this case, the women's movement. However, the third wave has largely been characterized as a young women's movement, and the generation gap has been played up as an explanation for ideological or strategic differences. The recognition of the cultural shift does not suggest that adult education and women's studies should become devoid of collective identity and move toward other structures. What it does suggest is that we need to consider broader societal changes and perspectives regarding social movement organizing and consider that these perspectives will be reflected in our students.

Schneirov and Geczik (1996) conducted ethnographic studies of alternative health networks, and they conceptualize these networks as needing to be "understood on a strategic level—as goal oriented, preference maximizing actors" (p. 628). The focus is not on the future and creating utopian structures. Instead, the focus is on the here and now: developing tangible modes of day-to-day life and practice that promote autonomy. Submerged networks do not have the visibility that solidarity-based social movements have through publicity, demonstrations, or public engagement with representatives of the status quo. Yet they are able to generate a sustained critique of a system, evidenced by consistent, daily actions that subvert and ultimately change the system. In other words, their focus is on changing cultural codes from the bottom up and bottom out. This practice, as described in Schneirov and Geczik's ethnographic study, is similar to the desire of many adult education graduate students who reject the label and perhaps even the political agenda of feminists and the feminist movement but want to dedicate their studies and practice to the improvement and betterment of women's lives through a focus on everyday practices within their thematic sphere. It also connects to current student interests in explicit connection of theory to daily educational practices.

Culture of "Public Experience of Self" Through Narration

The balance and tension between the individual and collective perspectives within adult education and women's studies is also influenced by the larger picture of general and social movements beyond the academy. McDonald (2002) posits that social movement actors can become caught up in the moment and in their own cultural webs, particularly with the advent of new media. Video, audio, photographic, and pop-culture forms of activism vividly capture "experiences" and propel individual examples of oppression and injustices into narrative forms. The popular Web site YouTube is an example of this process. The role of technology in creating a "public experience of the self" in relation to social issues is very compelling and leads to many unanswered questions. Adult education scholars have been slower than women's studies scholars to move to this type of cultural studies as a way to offer insight on larger adult education practice, although there are some contemporary scholars whose work examines social justice and social movement learning through contemporary public expression (Sandlin, 2005). Again, third-wave feminism (Baumgardner & Richards, 2000) promotes critical examination of creative forms of justice through multiple mediums and cultural studies. It is not revolutionary to state that adult education has been a little bit slow to examine more closely this aspect of feminist scholarship and practice. Although we are actively investigating the role of technology, cultural technology applications, and their roles in adult learning experiences, that discussion inhabits a separate sphere from most feminist and social movement scholarship.

Implications for Practice

This chapter is a brief exploration of a few of the issues that I believe exist for adult education graduate students who are interested in feminist scholarship and perhaps in the broader study of social justice. It suggests that interest alone is important but may be insufficient in drawing students into feminist and adult education integrated studies. The fact that women's studies and adult education have had long histories of praxis is no guarantee that they will continue that way. In order for students to sustain and thrive with a focus on social action, it is essential to observe students' responses to material and its relevance in their contexts. Although I have suggested that the patterns or reactions that I observe are problematic, it is not my intention to suggest that the students in our fields are problematic in their reactions or that all students interested in women's studies share the same approach. I believe that it is our job to reorient our perspective and ask what we can do to keep our fields of study current and relevant, without losing the feminist scholarship that has led us to this point.

If the fields of adult education and women's studies are sites of social movement learning and action and are also academic disciplines, then our students are already social movement participants. But we also need to continue to have dialogue with and learn from people in social movements that are external to academics. As such, a beginning discussion of future implications lies within three basic questions posed by Bevington and Dixon (2005):

1. What issues concern movement participants?
2. What ideas and theories are activists producing?
3. What academic scholarship is being read and discussed by movement participants?

If the scholarship that we as faculty members believe is most relevant is not reflected within these three questions, then we have a basis for further exploring why and how we can or should move existing theories into the praxis arena.

Notes

1. For more information on feminist activism within external organizations, see work by Roth (2004) on feminist activism in extrafeminist settings.

2. I draw on discussions with numerous adult education students at two different higher education institutions over 19 years of practice. Their ideas are paraphrased, and their real names and the names of their schools are not identified.

3. For an in-depth discussion and critique of the issue of the dual purpose of women's studies as an academic discipline and as a social movement, see Wiegman's Project MUSE "Academic Feminism Against Itself" (2002).

References

Baumgardner, J., & Richards, A. (2000). *Manifesta: Young women, feminism, and the future.* New York: Farrar, Straus, and Giroux.

Bevington, D., & Dixon, C. (2005). Movement-relevant theory: Rethinking social movement scholarship and activism. *Social Movement Studies, 4*(3), 185–208.

Boxer, M. J. (1998). *When women ask the questions: Creating women's studies in America.* Baltimore: Johns Hopkins University Press.

Cunningham, P. (2000). A sociology of adult education. In A. Wilson & E. Hayes (Eds.), *The handbook of adult and continuing education* (pp. 573–591). San Francisco: Jossey-Bass.

Hall, E., & Salupo Rodriguez, M. (2003). The myth of postfeminism. *Gender & Society, 17* (6), 878–902.

Hayes, E., & Flannery, D. (2000). *Women as learners: The significance of gender in adult learning.* San Francisco: Jossey-Bass.

Klatch, R. E. (2001). The formation of feminist consciousness among left- and right-wing activists of the 1960s. *Gender & Society, 15*(6), 791–815.

McDonald, K. (2002). From solidarity to fluidarity: Social movements beyond "collective identity": The case of globalization conflicts. *Social Movement Studies, 1*(2), 109–128.

Nelson, L. J., Shanahan, S. B., & Olivetti, J. (1997). Power, empowerment and equality: Evidence for the motives of feminists, nonfeminists, and antifeminists. *Sex Roles, 37*(3/4), 227–249.

Omolade, B. (2002). Women and work: Class within the classroom. *Women's Studies Quarterly, 30*(3/4), 284–293.

Ouellette, L. (1992, July/August). Our turn now: Reflections of a 26-year old feminist. *Utne Reader,* 118–120.

Roth, B. (2004). Thinking about challenges to feminist activism in extra-feminist settings. *Social Movement Studies, 3*(2), 147–166.

Sandlin, J. (2005). Culture, consumption and adult education: Refashioning consumer education for adults as a political site using a cultural studies framework. *Adult Education Quarterly, 55*(3), 165–181.

Schneirov, M., & Geczik, J. D. (1996). A diagnosis for our times: Alternative health's submerged networks and the transformation of identities. *Sociological Quarterly, 37*(4), 627–644.

Welton, M. (1987). Vivisecting the nightingale: Reflections on adult education as an object of study. *Studies in the Education of Adults, 19,* 46–68.

Wiegman, R. (2002). Academic feminism against itself. *National Women's Studies Association (NWSA) Journal, 14*(2), 17–37.

Wilson, A. L., & Hayes, E. (2000). On thought and action in adult and continuing education. In A. Wilson & E. Hayes (Eds.), *The handbook of adult and continuing education* (pp. 15–32). San Francisco: Jossey-Bass.

BACK(LASH) TO THE FUTURE

Jeanie K. Allen, Diane R. Dean, and Susan J. Bracken

In a July 2006 *New York Times* article, Tamar Lewin (2006) reported a growing concern that women are outnumbering and outperforming men at all levels of higher education. The number of women in higher education has exceeded the number of men for at least the past 40 years, but Lewin's report suggests that women exhibit more drive, come to class better prepared, worry more about grades, and demonstrate fewer tendencies to procrastinate and spend their time in leisure activities than their male counterparts do. Lewin suggests that women students desire to enter a career field and to establish themselves securely before committing to motherhood; in other words, women in higher education seem hungry for success and independence. However, Lewin also suggests that many male students feel that once they enter the work force, they will prevail, expressing a sense of entitlement and a recognition that the upper levels of the business world are still male dominated.

Some of the reactions expressed in Lewin's article suggest that this growth in women's academic achievement is creating a social crisis, almost reminiscent of comments from the 1950s indicating that women's education caused dissatisfaction and adjustment problems when they resumed their roles as housewives and mothers (Friedan, 1963/2001). In addition, several comments in the article hint that perhaps "normal" male behavior has now been labeled as problematic in the schools, thus discouraging male achievement. In response, the American Association of Colleges and Universities devoted an entire volume of *On Campus With Women* to an exploration of this so-called crisis, exposing the fallacies surrounding the "feminization" of higher education (Musil, 2007).

Caryn McTighe Musil, director of the Program on the Status and Education of Women for the Association of American Colleges and Universities, argues that the following assumptions have been made when supporting the idea that somehow education for women must be a zero-sum game:

- Equality for girls means inequality for boys.
- Equal numbers, or even above-equal numbers, means that equality has been achieved.
- Success for girls and women deprives boys and men of the chance of success.
- Girls and boys have no race or socioeconomic location.
- The missing boys and men in schools are white and middle or upper class. (Musil, 2007)

What most researchers have discovered is that race and socioeconomic status are much stronger factors in explaining differences in matriculation to college and degree attainment than gender, but the males-versus-females approach to the argument seems to garner the most press. In fact, it has been reported that several schools now use lower standards for accepting and admitting male students than they do for evaluating female applicants ("Admissions Are Now Biased Against Women," 2007). Although much has changed in higher education for women in the past 40 years, this implication that women's success in college somehow proves detrimental to men reminds us that gender roles and expectations still dominate societal perspectives.

This third volume in the Women in Academe series focuses on the current state of women's college experiences, both in and out of the classroom. We hope that we have presented both the contributions of scholars in the field and challenges that require future policy and research agendas. We know that each campus has its own set of challenges, but we continue to teach, serve, and research those areas of academe that might enhance learning for all. In this current economic environment, education beyond secondary schooling is becoming mandatory. We hope that this text has created curiosity on the part of the reader that fuels further interest and research into a variety of areas. Although feminist research and pedagogy has created some transformation of higher education, in policy, curriculum, and pedagogy, there is still much to be done. The intersection of gender, race, class, and sexual orientation still needs attention. The criticisms often voiced about higher education in general might also apply to the tendency for research on women in higher education to reflect the privileged, those who have access to universities and colleges. Much has been written about feminist pedagogy and the concerns that feminist educators have with power relationships, student empowerment, and maintaining an appropriate balance between experience and theory. We consider these issues to apply to all students, not just "the women."

Implications for Teaching, Learning, and Policy

Rather than distinguish between faculty and staff, we chose to address this last section to all members of academe whose job it is to assist students with their learning. The bridge between academic and student affairs still remains as a challenge to the student experience. In order for faculty to survive the tenure and promotion process, academe appears to require more and more specialization to assure publications and grants. This emphasis, however, may in fact harm faculty's concern for student learning. Unfortunately, prestige remains in the hands of those who research and publish significant works. We do not wish to undervalue this important contribution, but student learning must be given the same status and rewards that the more public sphere currently holds. The entire system, starting with doctoral education, needs to address the fact that many, if not most, faculty will find themselves in teaching-intensive institutions. Some graduate schools have now developed pathways and curricula to address teaching as a career; however, this track should become more equal to the research and publication track often more strongly promoted by the graduate faculty.

Accompanying this same train of thought, valid assessments of student learning must be developed and taken seriously. The evaluation process for publications is clear. Journals have been ranked, and there is an entire system of peer review designed to address what constitutes valid research contributions. With regard to student learning, faculty must engage in the difficult questions surrounding appropriate outcomes from a college education, so that the same level of judgment can be applied and compared. If we take seriously what we know about learning, and much of the new knowledge that has been created by studying women's experiences, we know that multiple-choice exams will not answer the myriad questions surrounding education outcomes. Student evaluation may constitute one of the largest challenges facing faculty and student-affairs professionals in the 21st-century institutions of higher learning.

In addition, we in higher education must design new systems that unite student- and academic-affairs personnel. Student learning happens in and out of the classroom, and the research in this text suggests that students seek an integration of their personal and academic lives. We cannot provide experiences to address students' desire for such integration unless we integrate student and academic affairs. Some institutions have designed partnership programs, but these are often seen in first-year-experience programs and not continued throughout the students' tenure at the college or university. Students model what they experience in our institutions. If we cannot integrate our working environments, then it will remain difficult for us to provide students with integrative experiences. This suggestion carries numerous implications for the structure that we place on higher education "units" and for the way we evaluate different personnel in different ways. It also speaks to the rewards and recognition systems that currently serve colleges and universities. Designing and implementing rich and integrated learning experiences for students needs to be considered equivalent to the publication of certain types of articles. This may read as quite revolutionary, but feminist praxis emerges from the world of activism. Higher education will need to redesign appropriate workloads in accordance with a renewed value placed on student learning. Relegating student learning to a lower status maintains the old patriarchal system that may not work to our advantage in this age of accountability.

We also need to evaluate our policies for overt and covert discriminatory practices. From admissions to commencement, from hiring to promotion, we need to examine our own work environments and ask whether they model an open and inclusive set of procedures. We must answer questions about the ways in which we have opened the doors for women and other underrepresented groups, while maintaining structures that require these individuals to assimilate into old patriarchal standards. This examination will require open, honest, and collaborative dialogue with the promise of action. Institutions of higher education will have to answer these questions within their own context and to consider and reconsider their mission.

The outgrowth of questions and concerns that have arisen from and through the study of women, women's studies programs, and feminist praxis are not just about improving the lives of women. Feminist educators recognize that this entire endeavor is aimed at fundamental questions of who is best served by social programs, institutions, and societal practice as a whole. Most colleges and universities now claim mission statements that reflect inclusive and global concerns. Research for and about women has always carried the undercurrent of activism aimed at a more equitable set of practices for all individuals. In this series, Women in Academe, we have asked a variety of questions about women's positions and contributions as faculty, administrators, and students of higher education—and questions lie at the heart of feminist education.

Feminist pedagogy asks students to critique social structures and practices, creates experiences that connect students' lives to the curriculum, uses dialogue and collaboration, promotes the recognition of the political aspects of most actions, utilizes listening and understanding others' points of view as valid educational practices, encourages learners to construct and own their knowledge, and demonstrates ways students can apply their learning to social transformation (Mayberry, 1999). As colleges and universities wrestle with the complexities of higher education in and for the 21st century, we suggest that they create a set of goals and objectives that serve all of us well.

Thus, when you come to a fork in the road, take it!

References

Admissions now are biased against women. (2007, August). *Women in Higher Education, 16,* 4.

Friedan, B. (2001). *The feminine mystique.* New York: Norton. (Originally published 1963)

Lewin, T. (2006, July 9). The new gender gap: At colleges, women are leaving men in the dust. *New York Times.* http://www.nytimes.com/2006/07/09/education/09college.html?_r = 1&n = Top/Reference/Times%20Topics/People/L/Lewin,%20Tamar&oref = slogin Accessed October 20, 2007

Mayberry, M. (1999). Reproductive and resistant pedagogies: The comparative roles of collaborative learning and feminist pedagogy in science education. In M. Mayberry & E. C. Rose (Eds.), *Meeting the challenge: Innovative feminist pedagogies in action* (pp. 1–22). New York: Routledge.

Musil, C. M. (2007). Beyond gender fallacies. *On Campus with Women, 35*(3). http://www.aacu.org/ocww/volume35_3/director.cfm Accessed October 20, 2007

ABOUT THE EDITORS AND CONTRIBUTORS

Jeanie K. Allen is a visiting assistant professor in interdisciplinary studies at Drury University in Springfield, Missouri. In the fall of 2008, she will hold an interdisciplinary position at Drury in behavioral sciences and interdisciplinary studies. She holds a Ph.D. in higher education from Walden University, an M.Ed. from Drury University, a master of science in accounting from the University of Arkansas, and a B.A. in zoology from the University of Arkansas. Her research areas include women's psychosocial development in undergraduate education and when navigating life and work, organizational behavior in higher education, and adult learning in health care settings. Prior to her full-time faculty position, she served as director of academic advising and The First Year Experience program at Drury University.

Marcia B. Baxter Magolda is a distinguished professor of educational leadership at Miami University of Ohio. She holds a Ph.D. in college student personnel/higher education and an M.A. in college student personnel/higher education from The Ohio State University, as well as a B.A. in psychology from Capital University. Her research interests stem from her 20-year longitudinal study of college students and include self-authorship, integrated perspectives of student and young-adult development, and learning partnerships as a model of creating learning environments. Her most recent books include *Learning Partnerships: Theory and Models of Practice to Educate for Self-Authorship,* published with Patricia King, and *Making Their Own Way: Narratives for Transforming Higher Education to Promote Self-Development.* She has received numerous awards for her contributions to the field of epistemological development in undergraduate students.

Susan J. Bracken is an assistant professor of adult education at North Carolina State University. Her D.Ed. is from Pennsylvania State University, where she studied both adult education and women's studies. Her research interests include gender issues in adult and higher education and adult learning in organizational contexts, especially community engagement and community-university partnerships. She is currently the senior researcher on a

National Science Foundation–funded research project that provides faculty instructional development to community college faculty in North and South Carolina. Before joining North Carolina State University in 2004, she served as special assistant to the vice president for outreach at Pennsylvania State University.

Diane R. Dean is an assistant professor of higher education administration and policy at Illinois State University. She holds an Ed.D. and M.A. in higher education administration from Columbia University and a B.A. in English and American literature from the University of Maryland, College Park. Her research interests center on the topics of higher education leadership, governance, policy, planning, diversity, and philosophical questions about the purpose and process of higher education. Prior to her faculty appointment, she was executive administrator for finance and administration at Teachers College, Columbia University.

Adrienne D. Dixson is an assistant professor in the School of Teaching and Learning at Ohio State University. She received a Ph.D. in multicultural education from the University of Wisconsin–Madison, an M.A. in educational studies from the University of Michigan–Ann Arbor, and a B.A. in music theory and composition from The Dana School of Music of Youngstown State University. Her research areas include investigations of race and gender in education. She is currently working on a book on the educational experiences of African American children and recently published *Critical Race Theory in Education: All God's Children Got a Song* with co-editor Celia K. Rousseau, published by RoutledgeFalmer Press.

Crystal Gafford Muhammad is an assistant professor of educational leadership at East Carolina University. She earned a Ph.D. in education policy and a J.D. from the University of Virginia and a B.A. from Spelman College. Her research centers on the intersection of race, class, and gender in higher education. She is the author of *From Diplomas to Doctorates: The Success of Black Women in Higher Education and Its Implications for Equal Educational Opportunities for All,* published by Stylus, and "An Oasis Within a Desert Palace: Proving Sex Discrimination in the New Millennium" in the *National Women's Association Journal.*

Catherine Marienau is a professor and faculty mentor at the School for New Learning at DePaul University. She holds a Ph.D. in adult higher education and curriculum and instruction, an M.A. in social and philosophic foundations of education, and a B.A. in anthropology from the University of Minnesota. Her research interests include assessment of student learning, including prior learning assessment; women's psychosocial development; adult learners and community-based learning; and reflection and learning from experience-reflective practice. In the spring of 2008, she, along with co-editor Susan Reed, will publish a sourcebook for New Directions for Adult and Continuing Education, *Linking Adults with Community: Using the Tools of Community-Based Learning to Promote Civic Engagement.* She is also the co-author of the second edition of *Assessing Learning: Standards, Principles, and Procedures,* published by Kendall/Hunt.

Betsy Palmer is an associate professor of education at Montana State University. She holds a Ph.D. in higher education from the Pennsylvania State University, an M.Ed. in higher education administration: student affairs from Western Washington University, and a B.A. in psychology and sociology from Whitman College. Her research interests include college-student personal epistemology, innovative college teaching, and engineering education. She currently serves on the research team of a 4-year National Science Foundation grant to study engineering programs with excellent student outcomes. Her most recent publications include "Individual Domain-Specific Epistemologies: Implications for Educational Practice," with R. M. Marra, in *Knowing, Knowledge and Beliefs: Epistemological Studies Across Diverse Cultures,* edited by M. S. Khine and to be published by Springer; and, with C. H. Major, "Engendering the Scholarship of Problem-Based Learning," *International Journal of Scholarship of Teaching and Learning, 1*(2) (2007).

Becky Ropers-Huilman is a professor of educational policy and administration at the University of Minnesota. She holds a Ph.D. in educational administration and an M.A. in educational administration from the University of Wisconsin–Madison, as well as a B.A. in psychology and German from the University of Wisconsin–Eau Claire. Her research interests include feminist education, diversity and identity in higher education, and civic education. She is currently working on an forthcoming anthology on poststructural feminist analyses of policies and practices related to postsecondary education (with Elizabeth Allan and Susan Iverson) and a qualitative inquiry about the ways in which discourses associated with engagement, democracy, and student roles affect the educational experiences of change agents in academic environments. In addition, a chapter by Ropers-Huilman titled "Women Faculty and the Dance of Identities: Constructing Self and Privilege Within Community" appeared in 2007 in *Unfinished Business: Women, Gender, and the New Challenges of Higher Education,* edited by Judith Glazer-Raymo and published by Johns Hopkins University Press.

David Sadker is a professor at American University (Washington, DC) and, along with his late wife, Myra Sadker, gained a national reputation for work in confronting gender bias and sexual harassment. The Sadkers' book, *Failing at Fairness: How Our Schools Cheat Girls,* was published by Touchstone Press in 1995. David Sadker co-edited *Gender in the Classroom: Foundations, Skills, Methods and Strategies Across the Curriculum* (Lawrence Erlbaum, 2007), and he co-authored an introductory teacher-education textbook, *Teachers, Schools and Society* (8th ed., McGraw-Hill, 2008; 1st brief ed., McGraw-Hill, 2007), which is a national best seller. Sadker has directed more than a dozen federal education grants, authored six books and more than 75 articles in journals such as *Phi Delta Kappan, Harvard Educational Review,* and *Psychology Today.* He is currently working on a revised edition of *Failing at Fairness.*

Marilyn K. Simon is a professor of education and research at Walden University and the University of Phoenix, as well as president of Best-Prep, LLC. She earned a Ph.D. in mathematics education from Walden University. Her research areas include the study of mathematics education, multicultural education, and at-risk students. She is currently involved in the Responsibility Project, an educational program for children who live in the Tijuana Dump, and she mentors doctoral students. She recently published *Dissertation and Scholarly Research: Recipes for Success* and a Spanish version of *Math Start* for pre-K and kindergarten children.

Teri Sosa is an assistant professor of education at St. Joseph's University. She holds an Ed.D. in instructional technology from Northern Illinois University and an M.B.A. from Loyola University, Chicago. Her field, instructional technology, lags behind others when it comes to enfranchising members of nondominant populations. Issues of race, class, and gender, as well as issues raised by minority populations, are attended to as an afterthought (if at all). Therefore, the core of her research addresses this omission by examining the ways we produce and use technology for instruction. Issues such as the digital divide, the representation (both verbally and visually) of people of color and women when creating software, the best and most enfranchising practices in the technology classroom, and the "masculinization" of technology spaces all find a way into her research.

Kathleen Taylor is a professor in the Graduate School of Education at Saint Mary's College of California. She holds a Ph.D. in adult higher education from the Union Graduate School. Her research areas include adult development and learning, transformational learning, prior learning assessment, women's development, neuroscience and adult learning, and faculty development. She has recently published a chapter in the *Oxford Handbook of Adult Development and Learning,* edited by Carole Hoare (2006), and is co-editor of *The Neuroscience of Adult Learning* (Jossey-Bass, 2006). In addition, she is about to welcome her fifth grandchild, Naomi, to the world.